<u>Vera's</u> Fine <u>Butter</u> <u>Cookies</u>.

1 pound best butter, 5 eggs, 2 cups
of granulated sugar, 2 tea-spoons
of yeast powder, ½ wine-glass-ful
of good brandy, hand-ful of almonds ground fine, but need not
be blanched, flour enough to roll
flavor with vanilla. Put on the
ice over night, so it can be rolled
out easily, as it is fine, and rich.
Brush the tops with one or two
eggs stirred up, and then sprinkle
with the almonds mixed with cinna
mon and sugar. They must be
rolled very thin, and watched
carefully, so as not to burn.
Do <u>not</u> forget a pinch of salt.

THE
OREGON TRAIL
COOKBOOK

Leslie J. Whipple

— A Maverick Publication —

ISBN 0-89288-234-4
Library of Congress Catalog Card Number: 92-62430

Photographer – Stephen Ingham

Food Stylist – Leslie J. Whipple

Layout and Design – Bridget R. Wise

Covered wagon reprinted from Rick Steber's *Oregon Trail Souvenir Book.* Illustration by Don Gray.

To order the *Oregon Trail Cookbook,* contact Maverick Distributors at Drawer 7289, Bend, Oregon 97708
1-800-333-8046

Dedicated to the loving memory of my grand-
mothers, Mabel Isabel Distad Whipple and Ruth
Lillian Hovey Johnson.

Acknowledgments

I want to express my gratitude and appreciation to Jerry Crowley who made everything possible.

I also wish to thank:
>
> Stewart Whipple
> Colby Whipple
> Marcia J. Whipple
> Helen Hall
> Stephen Ingham
> Evangelia O'Dell
> Rick Steber
> Gary Asher
> Patricia Wied
> Johan Mathiesen
> Marjorie Braker

This book would not have been possible without the contributions and cooperation of many people who made their recipes, stories and expertise available to The Oregon Trail Cookbook. I wish to thank them all for their generosity.

The Oregon Trail Cookbook

BREADS 3

SOUPS & STEWS 17

VEGETABLES & SALADS 25

FISH & FOWL 33

MEATS & GAME 43

CAKES 55

COOKIES & CANDY 75

PIES & PASTRIES 85

PUDDINGS & DUMPLINGS 97

PRESERVES & PICKLES 109

REMEDIES & RECEIPTS 121

NORTHWEST CHEFS 129

INDEX 159

Introduction

The year 1843 marked the beginning of what became known as the "Great Migration" to the Oregon Country. Forced to leave all but the most essential belongings behind, thousands embarked on a journey fueled by their dreams and hopes of reaching the "Promised Land."

At the heart of this journey was the daily struggle to feed the family. Dependent on their limited provisions and what they could hunt and gather along the way, these pioneers relied on their ingenuity and adaptability to survive. This cookbook is a tribute to the spirit and strength of the many pioneers who endured hardship along the Oregon Trail and went on to establish homesteads in a land untested and new. The contributions of the Native Americans who shared their knowledge of the land and its bounty with the pioneers must also be acknowledged as significant to the survival of many.

When the initial call for Oregon Trail recipes went out to newspapers across the country, I was unprepared for the overwhelming response. Descendants of pioneer families were eager to share their family legends, memories and cherished recipes. Their generosity was unparalleled as they sent me original recipe journals in the beautiful script of their forebears. The touching stories of hard work and reward, survival and celebration made it clear that the contributions were of significant historical interest and should be reproduced with a minimum of changes. The stories and recipes found within the double-lined boxes are written as I received them, too charming to change. All other recipes are standardized in order to make them more familiar in format and easier to use. Originally I planned to test the recipes; however taste is subjective, and the addition of any modern ingredients would decrease the value of these recipes as historical documents. These recipes will be donated to the Oregon Historical Society for future reference and study.

The essence of this project is participation. Without the efforts and kindness of so many people this book could not have been written. In acknowledgment, I have tried to include at least one recipe or story from every contributor.

In addition to the recipes, I received many curious home remedies and folk treatments. Unlike the traveling apothecaries of the day, I cannot in good conscience recommend or guarantee the efficacy of the nostrums and correctives within. They are offered as an entertaining glimpse at the healing arts of the period.

Finally, the last chapter is designed to showcase the extraordinary bounty we currently enjoy in the Oregon Country. Pacific Northwest chefs have donated recipes highlighting the astonishing variety of foods farmed, raised and gathered in Oregon. They are a testament to the tremendous dedication of our pioneer predecessors. The Oregon Trail Cookbook celebrates the heritage and legacy of those who have made Oregon their home.

Route of the OregonTrail

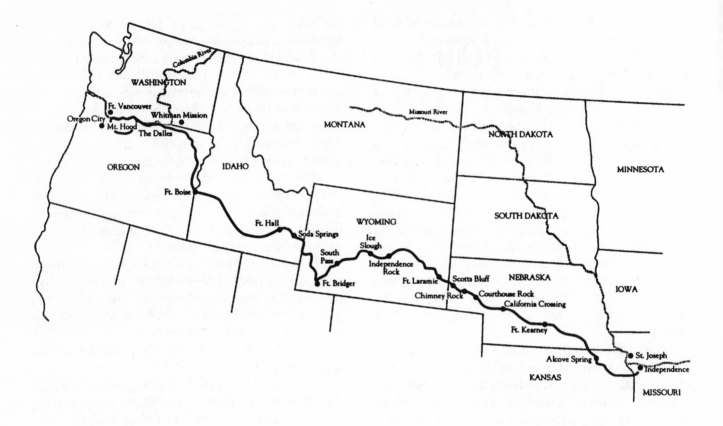

ST. JOSEPH, MISSOURI *GAZETTE*

MARCH 19, 1847

OUTFIT FOR OREGON

Mr. Editor; Subjoined you will find a list of the principle articles necessary for an outfit to Oregon or California, which may be useful to some of your readers. It has been carefully prepared from correct information derived from intelligent persons who have made the trip.

The wagons should be new, made of thoroughly seasoned timber, and well ironed and not too heavy; with good tight beds, strong bows, and large double sheets. There should be at least four yoke of good oxen to each wagon—one yoke to be considered as extra, and to be used only in cases of emergency. Every family should have at least two good milk cows, as milk is a great luxury on the road.

The amount of provisions should be as follows; to each person except infants:

200 pounds of bread stuff
(flour and crackers)

100 pounds of bacon
12 pounds of coffee
12 pounds of sugar

Each family should also take the following articles in proportions to the number as follows:

From 1 to 5 pounds tea
From 10 to 50 pounds rice
From ½ to 2 bushels beans
From ½ to 2 bushels dried fruit
From ½ to 5 pounds saleratus
From 5 to 50 pounds soap

Cheese, dried pumpkins, onions and a small portion of corn meal may be taken by those who desire them. The latter article, however, does not keep well.

No furniture should be taken, and as few cooking utensils as are indispensably needed. Every family ought to have a sufficient supply of clothing for at least one year after their arrival, as everything of that kind is high in those countries. Some few cattle should be driven for beef, but much loose stock will be a great annoyance. Some medicines should also be found in every family, the kind and quantity may be determined by consulting the family physician.

I would suggest to each family the propriety of taking a small sheet-iron cooking stove with fixtures, as the wind and rain often times renders it almost impossible to cook without them, they are light and cost but little. All the foregoing articles may be purchased on good terms in this place.

Kay Conn

My Mother's Recipe

While rummaging the other day
I found a treasure tucked away,
It was a faded recipe,
My mother once had given me.
I still recall the great delight,
When eating every luscious bite,
Of that grand cake of long ago,
None other can compare, I know.
I thought, I'll give my folks a treat,
With something really good to eat.
I hoped I could truly bake,
My mother's special chocolate cake,
But then, I read the recipe,
And more and more it stymied me!
"Take lots of flour," the paper said,
"The kind you use for making bread.
A scoop of sugar should be fine,
And with a lump of lard combine,
A dash of salt is all you need,
Just stir with ordinary speed,
Drop in an egg, or maybe two,
Pour in vanilla like I do,
Add milk until you've the right touch.
Put in enough but not too much,
The chocolate's better with milk sour,
Then bake for very near an hour."
Ah me, I'd love to bake that cake,
Again for my dear family's sake,
But I think mother willed to me,
A puzzle, not a recipe!

Marie Moore Hardin

Weights and Measures

1 teaspoon	=	⅓ tablespoon
1 tablespoon	=	3 teaspoons
4 tablespoons	=	¼ cup
¼ cup	=	12 teaspoons
Wineglass	=	¼ cup
Gill	=	½ cup
Teacup	=	½ cup
8 tablespoons	=	½ cup
16 tablespoons	=	1 cup
1 cup	=	½ pint
2 cups	=	1 pint
1 quart	=	2 pints
1 quart	=	4 cups
1 gallon	=	4 quarts
Butter the size of a walnut	=	2 tablespoons
Butter the size of an egg	=	4 tablespoons

Oven Temperature

Very Low Oven	=	250° to 275°
Low Oven	=	300° to 325°
Moderate Oven	=	350° to 375°
Hot Oven	=	400° to 425°
Very Hot Oven	=	450° to 475°

Breads

GRANDMA HUBBARD'S BAKING POWDER BISCUITS

My grandparents, Mary Clara and David Riley Hubbard, had twelve children. David died in 1928 and Mary Clara died in 1948. For many years before her death the local newspapers would run an article on her as one of the oldest residents in the area. From the Silverton Appeal of November 21, 1947 . . . "The nonagenarian still enjoys a clear recollection of early Oregon days. Her chief daily pleasure is preparing her own biscuits for breakfast."

2 cups flour
4 teaspoons baking powder
2 teaspoons sugar
½ teaspoon salt
½ teaspoon cream of tartar
½ cup shortening or lard
⅔ cup milk
1 tablespoon butter, melted

Preheat oven to 450 degrees.

Sift flour, baking powder, sugar, salt and cream of tartar together into a large mixing bowl. Cut the shortening in with a pastry cutter or fork until the mixture resembles coarse meal. Make a well in these ingredients and pour in the milk. Stir just until mixture forms a ball. Turn out onto lightly floured board and pat out until ½ to ¾-inch thick. Cut out biscuits with a floured 4-inch cookie cutter. Put melted butter in a pie pan. Dip each biscuit in the melted butter, turn over and arrange in the pie pan. Bake for 15 to 20 minutes or until golden brown.

Clara M. Foster

CLARA HAWKINS MOORE'S APPLE ROLLS

My great-great-great-grandparents, Henry and Martha Crafton Hawkins, were Oregon Pioneers of 1845. They were part of a 28 wagon caravan led as far as Fort Boise by Samuel Hancock. At Fort Boise some of the migration elected to join the Stephen Meek and Sol Tetherow parties who ventured across Eastern Oregon to become known as "the lost wagon train of 1845". Many lives were lost. Thomas Read, known by his contemporaries as a prudent and conservative man, chose to bring the Hawkins family with the others who remained on the established trail. This led them through Burnt River canyon and the Blue Mountains, to the Columbia.

1½ cups flour
3 teaspoons baking powder
1 teaspoon salt
2 tablespoons shortening
½ cup milk
Apples; peeled, cored and chopped
4 tablespoons butter, cut into small pieces
2 or 3 teaspoons cinnamon

Syrup:
1 cup sugar
2 cups boiling water
3 tablespoons butter
Cream as an accompaniment

Preheat oven to 350 degrees. Grease a 13x9x3-inch baking dish.

In a large bowl, sift together flour, baking powder and salt. Cut in shortening until mixture resembles coarse meal. Make a well in the center and add milk all at once. Stir just until dough forms. Turn onto a lightly floured board and knead lightly about 15 times. Roll out into a rectangle, three times long as wide. Cover with chopped apples. Dot with butter and sprinkle with cinnamon. Roll up, like cinnamon rolls, and cut into 1½-inch thick slices.

Stir syrup ingredients together until sugar is dissolved. Pour into prepared baking dish and place Apple Rolls in the syrup. Bake for about 25 minutes, or until golden brown. Serve hot with cream.

Hugh H. Hughes

Soda Bread

To make dough, mix 1 teaspoon of baking soda with 1 cup of warm water, add 2¼ cups of flour and 1 teaspoon salt. Knead well. The dough may be used at once or allowed to rise overnight in a warm place. In either case, flatten dough to a thickness of 1-inch. Place on a greased cookie sheet and bake in a 400 degree oven for about 25 minutes.

Lynda Hatch

NARCISSA'S CAMP BREAD

Narcissa Whitman and her husband Marcus came west over what was to become the Oregon Trail. Cooking out in the open over a campfire with only the most basic of cooking implements proved to be somewhat of an adventure to those enduring men and women who crossed this country in the early years of the great westward migrations.

As one of the first white women to undertake the journey of crossing the Rocky Mountains, Narcissa Whitman was thrust rather unprepared into this culinary excursion. Food provided not only the strength needed for the body to function but also gave an emotional comfort during difficult times. The diaries that Narcissa and some of the other missionary women kept during their extraordinary travels gives a glimpse of what their meals were like.

In a letter written to her sister on August 11, 1836 Narcissa gives the following instructions on how they might duplicate the bread she had just eaten, ". . . Had a present tonight of a fresh salmon, also a plate of fried cakes from Mr. McLeod. (Girls if you wish to know how they tasted you can have the pleasure of taking a little flour and water and make some dough and roll it thin, cut it into square blocks, then take some beef fat and fry them. You need not put either salt or pearl ash on your dough). Believe me I relish these as well as I ever did at home."

1 cup flour
½ cup water
Fat for frying; shortening, bacon fat,
     beef tallow, etc.

Mix flour and water together. Stir and knead to form a dough free from lumps. Turn onto lightly floured board and pat into a rough square about ½-inch thick. Cut into 2-inch squares.

Melt fat over medium heat in a heavy skillet or Dutch oven. Use enough to coat the bottom well. When hot, place a piece of dough in the fat. Cook until golden brown on both sides. Serve at once.

(The addition of 1½ teaspoons baking powder and ½ teaspoon salt to the dough will give our modern tastes a more palatable product).

June Cummins,
Park Ranger
Whitman Mission National Historic Site

Pinch-Offs

My ancestor, Allen Jones Davie II, came to Oregon in the early 1800s. He was one of the participants in the vote at Champoeg that made Oregon a part of the United States, rather than England. In 1844 he was married to Cynthia Ann Brown by Dr. David Leslie, in the Oregon City Territory.

The night before planning to bake the Pinch-Offs, mix about one-half cup sourdough starter with about one cup milk. Cover and set it in the wagon near the baby to keep warm. In the morning mix about one-half cup flour with three large pinches sugar, one pinch salt and about two pinches soda. Put about one-half cup flour on a board. Mix the dough really well, put on the floured board, knead a bit and pinch off pieces of dough, about the size of a baby's hand. Smear around in bacon grease or other melted fat. Put in a skillet. Cover and put near a warm spot for about one-half hour. Then, with the lid on, put close to the coals for about another one-half hour to bake.

Grandma Ball advises: "It will settle your stomachache if you will eat a couple big spoonfuls of the uncooked Spook Yeast." She meant the fermented sourdough sponge!

Anne Girod Foster

HOBO BREAD

3 cups raisins
4 teaspoons baking soda
2 cups water
4 cups flour
2 cups sugar
4 tablespoons oil
1 cup nuts, chopped

Preheat oven to 375 degrees. Grease 3 1-pound coffee cans or 3 9x5x3-inch bread pans.

In large bowl, combine raisins, baking soda and water and let stand for 1 hour. Stir in flour, sugar, oil and nuts to raisin mixture and blend well. Pour into prepared cans and bake for 1 hour.

Dorothy Winn Crawn

PRICILLA'S BOSTON BROWN BREAD

Original recipe from Pricilla Dean and John Alden, handed down in my family.

1 cup Indian meal (cornmeal)
1 cup graham flour
1 cup rye flour
1 cup whole wheat flour
1 cup unbleached white flour
1 cup dry bread crumbs
1 teaspoon salt derived from the sea
2 teaspoons baking soda
1 cup blackstrap molasses
3 cups sour milk or buttermilk
1 cup raisins or currants

Oil several cans; I use five number-2 cans.

In a large bowl, combine flours and salt. Dissolve baking soda in the molasses and add to the flour mixture. Stir in milk until well blended. Stir in raisins. Pour batter into prepared cans two-thirds full. Cover with foil and tie with string. Place on a rack in a steamer and fill with enough water to come halfway up sides of cans. Cover tightly and steam 3 hours. Remove from cans and cut by wrapping a strong linen thread (or string) around loaf, cross strings and pull. Good hot or cold, with butter or cheese.

Elinor Dean Pierce

Clotilda Deguire, third daughter of Francois Baptiste and Elenore St. Gemme Deguire was born August 17, 1854 in the Humbolt Sink area of Nevada as her parents were crossing the plains.

After her birth, the baby was placed in a basket on the back of the wagon. As the wagon bounced along the rutted trail, the basket and baby were pitched out of the wagon onto the trail.

Fortunately, the people in the wagon following saw and were able to stop before the oxen trampled the babe. They retrieved her, and that night when the wagons stopped for the day, she was returned no worse for the wear to her parents.

Clara M. Foster

Maryland Beaten Biscuit

Rub one tablespoon each of butter and lard into one quart of sifted flour, with one teaspoon of salt; gradually add milk enough to make a stiff dough, mixing it with the hand. When the dough is mixed, lay it on a floured bread board and beat it with the rolling pin, turning it continually, until it blisters and cracks loudly. It will require to be beaten about half an hour. When the blisters are abundant, tear off pieces of the dough as large as an egg, mold them in the form of a biscuit, prick the tops with a fork and bake in a rather quick oven.

Clara Kaneaster

AUNT TILLIE'S CINNAMON ROLLS

    1 cup mashed potatoes
    1 cup warm potato water (save water
        from boiled potatoes)
    ½ cup sugar
    ½ cup shortening
    2 eggs
    2 teaspoons salt
    2 packages yeast
    1 cup lukewarm water
    7 to 8 cups of flour

Cinnamon mixture:
    1 pound powdered sugar
    1 to 1½ sticks butter
    3 to 4 tablespoons cinnamon

Preheat oven to 350 degrees.

Mix mashed potatoes with potato water. In a separate bowl cream sugar and shortening. In a small dish beat eggs with salt. Dissolve yeast in lukewarm water. When dissolved, combine with potato mixture, creamed sugar and egg mixture. Gradually add flour and knead until dough reaches a workable consistency. Allow dough to refrigerate overnight if possible. Knead dough thoroughly and roll out dough to about ½ inch thick. Combine powdered sugar, butter and cinnamon. Spread cinnamon mixture over dough as if buttering bread. Carefully roll dough as if preparing a jelly roll. Cut dough into 1-inch sections and place in greased baking dishes. Let rise. Bake for approximately 30 minutes or until golden brown.

Helen Hall

BOSTON BROWN BREAD

    1 cup whole wheat flour
    1 cup rye flour
    1 cup cornmeal
    1½ teaspoons baking soda
    1½ teaspoons salt
    2 cups buttermilk or sour milk
    ¾ cup molasses
    1 cup raisins (optional)
    1 cup chopped nuts (optional)

Grease a 2-quart pudding mold.

Sift together dry ingredients into a large bowl. Stir in buttermilk and molasses until smooth. Stir in raisins and nuts if desired. Pour into prepared mold and cover tightly. Steam for 3½ hours.

Cynthia Berne

My grandmother, Mary Scott, related a story about her mother, Sarah Butler, who lived close to the Umpqua River where the Indians camped during the summers. After Sarah had baked her many loaves of bread, the Indians would walk into the house, uninvited, and help themselves to some of the bread. In the evening, they would return with dried and smoked fish and leave it on the table. Sarah came to expect the interruption without a word!

Irene Holcomb

GRANDMA MEACHAM'S HOT CAKES

Grandma Meacham served these every Sunday to her family and to the teamsters who slept at the Meacham Station on their way West.

Bacon
2 cups flour
1 tablespoon sugar
1 teaspoon baking soda

⅛ teaspoon salt
1 cup buttermilk
1 tablespoon oil
1 or 2 eggs, lightly beaten

Cook bacon on a hot griddle until desired crispiness. Drain on paper towels and set aside. Pour off all but 2 tablespoons bacon grease from griddle.

In a large bowl, sift flour, sugar, baking soda and salt. Add buttermilk, eggs and oil and stir until smooth. Spoon batter onto hot griddle and cook on both sides until golden brown. Serve with butter and maple syrup and the cooked bacon.

Elizabeth Redington Meacham Stewart

CRACKLING CORN CAKES

2 eggs, lightly beaten
1 cup buttermilk
2 tablespoons melted bear renderings
        (or melted bacon fat)
    2 cups cornmeal
    1½ teaspoons baking powder
    1 teaspoon salt
    ½ teaspoon baking soda
¾ cup bear cracklings,
    finely crushed
    (or crumbled cooked bacon)
2 tablespoons bear lard, for frying
    (or bacon fat)

Combine eggs, buttermilk and melted bear renderings in a large bowl. In a separate bowl mix together cornmeal, baking powder, salt and baking soda. Stir into first mixture until well combined. Stir in bear cracklings.

Heat bear lard in a frying pan over medium heat. Drop batter by tablespoons into frying pan, cook until golden brown, then turn and cook on the other side until nicely browned.

Irene Mead

Spider Corncake

This recipe is from my grandmother's collection. I have made it many times in a Dutch oven while camping with great success, and hardly a crumb remaining.

Measure out one and two-thirds cupfuls of cornmeal, one-third cupful of flour, one-fourth cupful of sugar and a teaspoon of salt. Sift all together and add to them two eggs which have been beaten with a cupful of sour milk and one of sweet milk in which a small teaspoon of soda has been dissolved. Stir all thoroughly. Put one or two tablespoons of butter in a hot spider on the fire. When the butter has melted, pour the batter into the spider, open the oven door and place the spider on the lower shelf. Pour another cupful of sweet milk into the batter but do not stir at all. Now shut the door and let the cake bake without touching it for about twenty minutes or half an hour in a quick oven. When a rich brown and done, lift the cake out of the pan and place on a large plate or cut into thick slices in the pan and serve hot with butter. The peculiar feature of this cake is that it has streaks of a creamy consistency running through the whole, especially near the bottom or top. This makes it delicious, and it is due to the cupful of milk added at the last moment, just before the oven is shut.

Susie Menefee

FRIED SODA BISCUITS

The range cook shaped soda biscuits by a different method than used today. Since he did not want to bother with a biscuit cutter, he merely pinched off pieces of dough about the size of an egg. He then rolled these pieces into balls with his hands and fried them in hot grease in the Dutch oven.

    2 cups flour
    1 teaspoon baking soda
    ½ teaspoon salt
    ¼ cup shortening
    ¾ cup buttermilk or sour milk
    Shortening for frying

Stir together flour, baking soda and salt. Cut in ¼ cup shortening until the mixture resembles coarse crumbs. Make a well in the dry mixture; add buttermilk or sour milk all at once. Stir just until the dough clings together. Knead gently on lightly floured surface 10 to 12 strokes. Melt enough short-ening in deep skillet to make 1-inch of melted shortening. Heat shortening to 375 degrees. To shape each biscuit, cut off about 1 tablespoon of the dough and form into a ball about 1-inch in diameter; flatten slightly. Carefully place biscuits, a few at a time, in the hot shortening. Fry until golden, turning once, about 2 minutes per side. Drain on paper towels. Serve hot. Makes about 24 biscuits.

Lynda Hatch

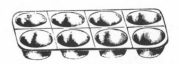

GRAM BATES' ROLLS

My husband, Bud, can still smell the rolls his Grandma Bates would be taking out of the oven as he and his five sisters came home from school. Simple, but so good!

    2 cups warm water
    1 package active dry yeast
    1 teaspoon salt
    ¼ cup oil
    5 to 6 cups flour
    Butter

Preheat oven to 350 degrees. Butter a baking sheet.

Dissolve yeast in warm water and allow to proof. Add salt and oil. Stir in enough flour to make a soft dough that can be kneaded. Turn out dough onto a lightly floured board, and knead for several minutes until resilient. Let raise until doubled in bulk. Punch down. Form rolls and arrange on a buttered baking sheet about ½-inch apart. Allow to raise until doubled in bulk. Bake for approximately 15 to 20 minutes or until nicely browned. As soon as rolls are taken from the oven, rub tops with butter.

Jacqueline Mitchael

GRANDMA FAYE'S HOT ROLLS

½ cup lukewarm water
1 package yeast
1 cup lukewarm water
1 tablespoon salt
2 tablespoons sugar
2 tablespoons oil
4 to 5 cups flour

Preheat oven to 375 degrees.

Combine ½ cup lukewarm water with yeast and set aside to proof. In a large bowl, combine 1 cup lukewarm water, salt, sugar and oil. Stir in about 2 cups of flour or enough to make a soft sponge. Stir in the yeast mixture and beat vigorously with a wooden spoon. Beat in remaining flour to make a stiff dough. Turn out onto a lightly floured board and knead until smooth. Cover, put in a warm place and let rise until doubled in bulk. Punch down and roll out to a thickness of ½-inch. Cut out with a round 2½-inch cutter and place on a buttered baking sheet. Cover and let rise for 1 hour. Bake for about 20 minutes, or until golden brown.

Donice Brashear
Betsy Krause

Mormon Johnnycake

Combine two cups of yellow cornmeal, ½ cup flour, 1 teaspoon baking soda and 1 teaspoon salt. Stir in two cups of buttermilk and two tablespoons of molasses. Pour batter into a greased 9-inch pan and bake in a 425 degree oven for about twenty minutes. Cut into 16 squares. To make lighter cake; add two beaten eggs and two tablespoons of melted butter to buttermilk and cook about 25 minutes.

Lynda Hatch

Tea Biscuits

Mix 1 cup butter, 1 cup milk, 4 eggs, 3 cups flour 1 teaspoonful salt, 1½ teaspoonsful soda and 2 teaspoonsful cream of tartar. Make into a thin loaf and bake in a flat greased pan. Break into chunks. Serve warm with butter and honey.

Lynda Hatch

RHUBARB BREAD

1 egg, beaten
1½ cups brown sugar
1 cup buttermilk or sour milk
½ cup oil
1 teaspoon vanilla
2½ cups flour
1 teaspoon baking soda
1 teaspoon salt
1½ cups rhubarb, finely diced
½ cup nuts, chopped
Zest from 1 orange, minced

Preheat oven to 350 degrees. Grease two 9x5-inch loaf pans.

In a large bowl beat the egg and brown sugar together. Stir in buttermilk, oil and vanilla. Sift flour, baking soda and salt together and gradually stir into mixture. Fold in rhubarb, nuts and orange zest. Pour into prepared pans and bake about 40 minutes, or until toothpick inserted in the center comes out clean.

Virginia A. Whipple

SPUDNUTS

Bet you can't eat just one!

1 cup shortening
2 tablespoons warm mashed potatoes
1 egg, separated
⅓ cup sugar
2 teaspoons salt
1 quart milk, warmed
2 packages dry yeast
½ cup lukewarm water
9 to 10 cups flour
Oil for frying

Glaze:

1 pound powdered sugar
2 tablespoons vanilla
Few drops water

In a large bowl, cream together the shortening and potatoes. Beat egg white until stiff then fold into the potato mixture. Beat egg yolk, sugar and salt together until thick, then add to mixture and beat until fluffy. Heat milk until lukewarm, add yeast and warm water then stir until yeast dissolves. Add to mixture and stir to blend. Add enough flour to make a soft dough. Cover and let rise 1½ to 2 hours, or until doubled in bulk.

Punch down and divide dough into thirds. Roll out on floured board to a thickness of ½ inch. Cut with a floured doughnut cutter and let rise until doubled in bulk. Heat 2 inches oil to 370 degrees. Put doughnuts in the hot oil, a few at a time, and fry until golden brown, then turn to brown on the other side. Remove and drain on absorbent paper towels.

Mix powdered sugar and vanilla together. Add enough water, a few drops at a time, to make a thick paste. Spread on warm doughnuts.

Janice M. Hardy

JOLLY BOYS

My grandmother first saw my grandfather when she was traveling in a covered wagon. She looked out the back and watched this cowboy, and thought "how interesting and good-looking". They eventually married and had five boys and five girls.

1 package active dry yeast
¼ cup warm water, 105 degrees to 115 degrees
1 cup milk, scalded
¼ cup butter
1 tablespoon sugar
1 teaspoon salt
2 eggs, beaten
1 cup cornmeal
2 cups flour
Oil for frying

Dissolve yeast in the warm water, set aside. Pour scalded milk into a large mixing bowl then add butter to hot milk and stir to melt. Stir in sugar and salt and let cool. Add eggs and yeast and stir to combine. Stir in the cornmeal then the flour.

Cover and let rise until doubled in bulk. Stir down and allow to rise again.

Heat oil to 360 degrees. Disturbing the batter as little as possible, drop by large spoonfuls into the hot oil. Cook until golden brown then drain on absorbent paper. Keep warm until all Jolly Boys are cooked. Serve warm with butter.

Sandra L. Stanley

10

CHURCH BAZAAR DOUGHNUTS

This recipe is said to have been used by pioneer women who came west on the wagon trains. It is unique in that the doughnuts become rather 'creamy' in taste as they age, if kept in airtight containers.

>2 cups sugar
>4 eggs
>4 tablespoons melted butter
>1¼ teaspoons baking soda
>1½ cups buttermilk
>4 to 6 cups flour
>Oil for frying

Cream together the sugar, eggs and melted butter. Dissolve baking soda in the buttermilk and stir into sugar mixture. Add just enough flour to make a soft dough that can be easily handled. Cover dough and let rest for at least four hours.

Heat at least 2-inches of oil to 370 degrees. Pat the dough out on a floured board and cut with a floured doughnut cutter. Put doughnuts, a few at a time, into the hot oil and fry until golden brown, then turn to brown on the other side. Remove and drain on absorbent paper towels.

Betty Jo Bauman (Mrs. R.H.)

LUMBER CAMP DOUGHNUTS

>1 package active dry yeast
>¼ cup warm water, 105 degrees to 115
>   degrees
>1 cup brown sugar
>4 eggs
>1 cup evaporated milk
>1 cup warm water
>⅔ cup bear grease or lard or shortening,
>   melted
>2 teaspoons salt
>4 cups flour
>Oil for deep frying

Place yeast in a large mixing bowl, add the ¼ cup warm water and stir. Add sugar and mix well.

Let stand 10 minutes to proof. Add eggs, evaporated milk, remaining water, bear grease, salt and flour. Stir vigorously with a wooden spoon until dough is springy. Cover and let rise until doubled in bulk. Punch down and turn out onto a floured board. Roll out half the dough at a time to a thickness of approximately ¾-inch. Cut with a floured doughnut cutter. Cover and let rise until doubled in bulk.

Heat 2 or more inches of oil to 370 degrees. Put the doughnuts in, a few at a time, top sides down. Cook until nicely browned, then turn over to brown on the other side. Drain on absorbent towels.

Sandra L. Stanley

My great-great-grandmother, Martha Jane Mays, was nineteen years old when she married John Mays in 1851 in Missouri. They set out for Oregon in an oxen-drawn covered wagon in May of 1852. They arrived in the Yamhill County in October, taking up a land claim about three miles south of present-day McMinnville. This is her account of what they ate that first winter for survival:

"There were a few farmers who had raised small fields of wheat that went [from] $3.00 to $5.00 per bushel before we were able to buy; so we could only buy enough to boil, glad to have that, in fact. In fact, we became very fond of boiled wheat, it tasted so strong of money. . . . We had one milk cow and we lived on milk and what butter I could make. There was [only] my husband and myself to feed, so by economizing closely we lived through the first winter."

They later had ten children, and moved to the Umatilla County area where quite a number of their descendants still live.

Helen B. Woodroofe

MOM'S BUTTERMILK HUCKLEBERRY PANCAKES

6 eggs, separated
1⅔ cups buttermilk
1 teaspoon baking soda
1½ cups flour
1 teaspoon baking powder
½ teaspoon salt
¼ cup butter, melted and cooled
1 tablespoon sugar
2 cups huckleberries

Lightly beat egg yolks in a large mixing bowl. Dissolve baking soda in buttermilk and add to egg yolks. Sift together flour, baking powder and salt and gently fold into mixture just enough to moisten. Gently fold in melted butter and set aside. Beat egg whites until soft peaks form then add sugar and continue beating until stiff. Fold egg whites gently into batter and stir in huckleberries. Batter should be lumpy.

Heat a griddle to medium high—about 350 degrees. Grease lightly and pour about ¼ cup of batter per pancake. Cook until a few bubbles break on top and bottom is golden brown. Turn the pancakes over and cook until bottom is golden brown. Keep warm and serve with butter and maple syrup.

Marcia Joan Hovey Johnson Whipple

NANA'S CORNBREAD

½ cup sugar
⅓ cup shortening
2 eggs
1 cup buttermilk
1 teaspoon baking soda
¾ cup cornmeal
2 teaspoons baking powder
1 teaspoon salt
1 cup flour

Preheat oven to 350 degrees and grease a 9x9-inch pan.

In a mixing bowl, cream together the sugar and shortening. Add the eggs one at a time, beating well after each addition. Dissolve baking soda in the buttermilk and stir into mixture. In a separate bowl combine cornmeal, baking powder and salt. Add to mixture and stir until well blended. Add flour and stir well.

Pour into prepared pan. Bake for 20 minutes or until toothpick inserted in the center comes out clean.

Mabel Isabel Distad Whipple

SOURDOUGH CORNBREAD

1 cup sourdough starter
1½ cups cornmeal
1½ cups milk
2 eggs, lightly beaten
2 tablespoons sugar
¼ cup bacon drippings, melted
¾ teaspoon baking soda
½ teaspoon salt

Preheat oven to 400 degrees. Lightly grease a 10 inch cast-iron frying pan.

In a large mixing bowl combine sourdough starter, cornmeal, milk, eggs and sugar until smooth. Stir in bacon drippings, baking soda and salt until well combined. Pour into prepared pan and bake for about 25 minutes or until toothpick inserted in the center comes out clean.

Irene Mead

WHOLE WHEAT QUICK BREAD

Phoebe Elizabeth Cook Hale served as hair-dresser and assistant to the cook in the royal house-hold of Queen Victoria. She brought this recipe with her to Mormon country and it has been handed down in her family.

2 cups buttermilk
1 egg, beaten
3 tablespoons molasses or honey
1½ tablespoons butter, melted
2 cups whole wheat flour
1 teaspoon baking powder
1 teaspoon baking soda
1 teaspoon salt
½ cup raisins
½ cup nuts, chopped

Preheat oven to 400 degrees. Grease two 9x5-inch loaf pans.

Combine buttermilk, egg, molasses and butter in a large mixing bowl. Sift together whole wheat flour, baking powder, baking soda and salt then stir into mixture. Stir in raisins and nuts. Divide batter between the two pans. Bake 50-60 minutes or until toothpick inserted in the center comes out clean.

J. Mitchell Russell

NOODLES

Break 2 eggs in a bowl. Add some salt. Add 2½ eggshells of cream. Put in flour to make a stiff dough. Cover and let set for a while, about as long as it takes to sweep and dust. Roll thin, cut and hang on broom handle which has been placed on the backs of dining room chairs. Use when dry.

J. Mitchell Russell

NOODLES

1½ cups flour
2 eggs, lightly beaten
1½ tablespoons cream
½ teaspoon salt

Sift flour into a large bowl and make a well in the center. Combine eggs, cream and salt and pour into the well. Stir together with a fork until dough is soft but not sticky. Turn out on a lightly floured board and knead until smooth and satiny, about 7 minutes. Cover and let rest for about 30 minutes.

On a lightly floured board, roll out dough to approximately ⅛-inch thick. Cut noodles to desired thickness and hang to dry on a broom handle which has been suspended between the backs of two dining room chairs.

J. Mitchell Russell

SCONES FROM FORT VANCOUVER

7½ cups flour
3 tablespoons baking powder
¾ cup butter
2½ cups sugar
1½ cups currants
2½ cups light cream
1 egg, beaten

Preheat oven to 375 degrees. Lightly oil a baking sheet.

Sift flour and baking powder together into a large bowl. Cut in butter until mixture resembles coarse meal. Stir in sugar and currants. Stir in light cream until dough is formed. Roll out onto a lightly floured board until ½ to ¾-inch thick. Cut out with a biscuit cutter and brush tops with beaten egg. Bake for 10 to 15 minutes.

Rick Edwards
Park Ranger
Fort Vancouver National Historic Site

Dutch Oven Cooking

Have two fires going in camp; one for cooking and a campfire. Preheat Dutch oven lid. Put cornbread batter or baking powder biscuit dough in Dutch oven and cover with pre-heated lid. Cover lid with about 1½-inches of hot coals. Be careful not to scoop dirt or ashes onto lid since they will insulate against the heat getting to the lid. Then put some hot coals on the ground and set lidded oven on top. Turning the lid and the oven several times ensures uniform cooking.

Bob Pruitt

Fried Cakes

Combine 1½ cups of flour with one cup of water. Mix well with a fork. Using plenty of flour on hands and breadboard, roll out dough to a thickness of ¼-inch. Cut into 2-inch squares. Render beef fat in a skillet and add squares of dough. Brown slowly on both sides. Sprinkle with salt to taste. Makes about 20 cakes.

Lynda Hatch

Soups & Stews

CAYUCAS BEANS

1 pound dry kidney beans
1 meaty ham bone
2 medium onions, quartered
5 stalks celery, cut into 1-inch pieces
1 large green bell pepper, chopped
4 to 5 cloves garlic, minced
1 teaspoon salt
1 teaspoon pepper
½ teaspoon cayenne pepper

Cover beans with water overnight. Drain beans then put in a large pot with remaining ingredients and barely cover with water. Cover pot and simmer over low heat for about 1½ hours or until beans are very tender.

Helen Nelson

OXTAIL SOUP

2 oxtails
4 quarts water
3 tablespoons flour
2 slices bacon, diced
2 onions, chopped
2 carrots, sliced
1 turnip, diced
2 stalks celery, sliced
3 green peppers, diced
2 whole cloves
1 teaspoon salt
¾ cup sherry
1 tablespoon cornstarch

FISH CHOWDER

1 pound fresh halibut or cod
1 quart water
2 cups potato, diced
1 onion, sliced thinly
1 teaspoon salt
1 cup whipping cream
2 tablespoons butter

In a large pot simmer fish in water over low heat until just tender. Add potato, onion and salt and simmer until very tender. Stir in cream and butter and heat through, do not let boil. Serve with crackers.

Jo Anne Brown

Disjoint oxtails and place in large pot. Add water and simmer over low heat about 2 hours, skimming off fat occasionally. Remove oxtails with slotted spoon and pat dry. Dredge in flour. Cook bacon in a large frying pan until crisp, then brown the oxtails well in the bacon fat. Remove oxtails and bacon from frying pan and return to pot. Sauté the onions, carrots, turnip and celery in frying pan until tender, then add to pot. Add peppers, cloves and salt to pot then simmer over low heat 1 hour, skimming off fat occasionally. Stir sherry and cornstarch together then stir into soup. Cover and simmer over low heat for 4 more hours.

Jo Anne Brown

TOMATO STEW WITH DUMPLINGS

1 medium onion, finely chopped
2 tablespoons butter
6 large tomatoes, chopped or 2½ cups
       canned tomatoes
1 teaspoon salt
½ teaspoon sugar
Dash of pepper

Dumplings:
1 cup flour
2 teaspoons baking powder
½ teaspoon salt
Pinch of paprika
2 tablespoons butter
½ cup milk

Heat butter in a large pot over medium heat. Add chopped onion and sauté until translucent. Add tomatoes, salt, sugar and pepper and simmer over medium-low heat for 10 minutes, stirring occasionally.

For the dumplings, stir the dry ingredients together then work in the butter with a fork until blended. Add the milk and stir to make a soft dough. Drop by tablespoonfuls into the stew. Cover and simmer 10 minutes. Serve immediately.

Louise O'Dea

AUNT HATTIE'S OYSTER STEW

2 cups celery, thinly sliced
1½ cups water
1 teaspoon salt
¼ teaspoon pepper
4 cups milk
4 tablespoons butter
5 cups oysters
Parsley

In a large sauce pan, combine celery, water, salt and pepper and simmer until tender. Add milk, butter and oysters and simmer over low heat until oysters are cooked. Do not boil. Serve hot, garnished with minced parsley.

Jo Anne Brown

Mulligan Stew

This recipe is from my grandfather, George Greenwood Bingham (1855-1924), who even after heart trouble went deer hunting with his friends although he remained in camp as the cook.

Take part of the backbone of a deer, leaving in back straps. Boil in stock from the soup can. When nearly done add potatoes and onions cut in rather small pieces. Salt and pepper to taste.

G. Bingham Powell

ROSEMABAWLER (Potato Dumpling Soup)

My great-grandfather, Ole Christiansen, came from Norway to settle in Wisconsin. He found so many others named Christiansen that he changed his name to Rodby. Where he got that name, no one knows. He married Margaret Doostaad and came to Oregon, where they had thirteen children. This rich soup is from Margaret and is traditionally served with a glass of tomato juice to drink as an accompaniment.

    1 meaty ham hock
    1 quart water
    8 medium potatoes, peeled and grated
    Flour to bind the potatoes
    Melted butter

Cook the ham hock in the water until the meat falls off the bone. Strain the stock and skim the fat from the stock. Combine the grated potatoes with enough four until the mixture holds together. Drop the dumplings by the tablespoonful into barely simmering stock. Cover and simmer gently for about 1 hour.

Serve dumplings with melted butter on platter with pieces of ham. Serve broth as a dinner soup.

Sally (Springer) Madden

GRANDMA PARKER'S FRUIT SOUP

Grandma Parker was the daughter of one wife of a polygamist marriage. She came to Utah as a child, traveling with her sister and her parents across the country from Minnesota. They didn't even have a covered wagon. They walked pulling their meager possessions in a hand cart.

This soup was served to anyone recovering from the flu or a bad cold.

    10 to 12 dried prunes
    10 to 12 dried apricots
    ⅓ cup raisins
    1 stick cinnamon
    1 whole cardamom
    2 slices lemon
    ¼ cup brown sugar
    2 tablespoons quick-cooking tapioca
    1 apple; peeled, cored and chopped

Place prunes, apricots and raisins in a large sauce pan. Cover with cold water and soak for 1 hour. Add cinnamon, cardamom, lemon, brown sugar and tapioca. Cover and simmer over low heat, stirring occasionally, for about 20 minutes, or until tender. Stir in apple and simmer additional 10 minutes. If soup is too thick, thin with water or fruit juice. Remove cinnamon and cardamom then puree. Serve hot to the recovering, or cold as a dessert.

Judith Massee

YOGURT MUSHROOM SOUP

4 tablespoons butter
¾ pound mushrooms, thinly sliced
1 medium onion, chopped
6 green onions, sliced
¼ cup flour
2 teaspoons paprika
½ teaspoon garlic salt
6 cups chicken broth
1½ cups yogurt
2 egg yolks, lightly beaten
¼ teaspoon dill

Melt butter in a large pot. Add mushrooms, onion and green onion and sauté over medium heat until limp. Stir together flour, paprika and garlic salt then stir into the mushroom mixture. Whisk in chicken broth gradually. Reduce heat to medium-low and simmer 30 minutes. Blend yogurt, egg yolks and dill. Stir ½ cup of soup into yogurt mixture. Stir yogurt mixture into the soup. Heat through but do not let boil.

Lorraine Heller

GRANDMA MARION'S BAKED BEANS

1 pound small white beans
1 teaspoon baking soda
½ cup brown sugar
¼ cup sugar
⅓ cup molasses
1 teaspoon dry mustard
1 large onion, chopped
5 to 6 slices uncooked bacon, cut up
½ cup catsup
Salt to taste

Preheat oven to 300 degrees.
Soak beans and baking soda in enough water to cover, overnight. Rinse beans. Put beans in a large oven proof pot and cover with water. Parboil until the skins break. Add brown sugar, sugar, molasses, dry mustard, onion and bacon. Cover and bake for about 4 hours. Add catsup and salt and continue baking for an additional 1 to 2 hours, or until tender. Yum!

Jacqueline Wilson

BOSTON BAKED BEANS

This recipe is from my great-grandmother, Mary Jane Stevens, who came across the Oregon Trail in 1852.

3 cups dried beans
1 teaspoon baking soda
3 tablespoons molasses
2 tablespoons sugar
2 teaspoons salt
½ teaspoon dry mustard
½ pound bacon
1 onion, peeled

Preheat oven to 300 degrees.
Soak beans overnight in water to cover. Drain off water. Cover again with water and add baking soda. Parboil until the skins break. Drain and rinse with boiling water. Put beans into large bean pot or oven-proof pot. Add molasses, sugar, salt and dry mustard. Lay bacon and whole onion on top. Add 1 cup boiling water. Cover pot and bake for 5 to 6 hours or until done. Add boiling water if they get dry.

Cynthia Berne

SPLIT PEA SOUP

Leslie and Amelia Hatfield came from Kansas in the spring of 1890 to build a homestead on North Deer Creek in the Roseburg, Oregon area. The home they built still stands. This is a recipe from their daughter, Marion Hatfield, who was a true pioneer lady.

7 cups water
3 cups green split peas
1 large onion, chopped
1 cup celery, chopped
1 medium carrot, grated
4 cups milk
½ cup cooked bacon, crumbled
Salt to taste

Combine water, split peas, onion, celery and carrot in a large pot. Simmer for about 45 minutes. Stir in the milk, bacon and salt and reheat. Serve hot.

Jacqueline Wilson

ONION SOUP

2 tablespoons butter
2 large onions, chopped
2 tablespoons flour
1 quart milk
½ pound cheddar cheese, grated
1 teaspoon salt
½ teaspoon pepper
Croutons

Melt butter in a large sauce pan and sauté onions over medium-low heat until golden brown. Whisk in flour, then stir in milk, whisking constantly. When soup is hot, add cheese and stir until melted. Remove from heat and season with salt and pepper. Serve with croutons.

Jo Anne Brown

BLACK BEAN SOUP

½ pound black beans
2 quarts chicken stock
3 tablespoons butter
1½ cups carrots, sliced thinly
1 large onion, chopped
1 green pepper, chopped
1 cup fresh cilantro; lightly packed,
    then minced
4 cloves garlic, minced
1 cup dry white wine
3 teaspoons cumin
2 teaspoons chili powder
1½ teaspoons salt
1 teaspoon cayenne pepper
Sour cream
Green onions, chopped

Soak beans overnight in chicken stock. Put in a large pot, bring to a boil then reduce heat and simmer for 3 hours. Remove half of the beans, puree then return to the soup. Melt the butter in a large skillet and sauté the carrots, onion, green pepper, cilantro and garlic just until tender. Add vegetables, wine, cumin, chili powder, salt and cayenne pepper to the soup; cover and simmer for an additional hour. Serve with a dollop of sour cream and chopped green onion.

Doran Lynn Whipple

CREAM TOMATO SOUP

Lula Foster Schminck was the youngest of 15 children born to James Foster and Elizabeth Currier. James Foster was a member of the ill-fated wagon train which chose to follow Stephen Meek across the Eastern Oregon desert in 1845. Elizabeth Currier crossed the plains by way of the Applegate Trail in Southern Oregon in 1846. She and her sister were the first white women to pass through Canyon Creek Canyon. Her brother, Manley Currier, drove the first wagon through and her brother-in-law, A. L. Humphrey, was the only man who got through with a whole wagon and complete team. It was a nightmare.

4 cups milk
1½ tablespoons butter
1 tablespoon flour
⅛ teaspoon baking soda
1 cup tomato puree
Salt to taste
Dash of Worcestershire sauce, (optional)
1 tablespoon minced onion, (optional)

Put the milk in a large saucepan and bring to a boil. In a small bowl, mix the butter and flour together with a fork. Add a little of the hot milk to the butter mixture and whisk until smooth. Pour back into the pot, whisking constantly, and cook until slightly thickened. Add remaining ingredients and simmer until heated through.

Mrs. James H. (Teressa) Foster

Vegetables & Salads

RUBY ROYAL

James H. Foster recalls that his mother, Maybelle Hoy Foster, used to make this dish and it was very tasty.

2 cups canned tomatoes
1 small onion, finely chopped
3 tablespoons butter
1 teaspoon salt
⅛ teaspoon cayenne pepper
6 eggs
6 pieces buttered toast

Combine tomatoes, onion, butter, salt and cayenne in a medium saucepan and simmer over medium-low heat for 15 minutes. Strain and return tomato sauce to pan. Increase heat to medium. Carefully break eggs into the simmering tomato sauce without breaking the yolks and poach until firm. Serve at once by placing a poached egg with a spoonful of tomato sauce on each piece of buttered toast.

Mrs. James H. (Teressa) Foster

BAKED EGGPLANT

1 eggplant, peeled and cubed
½ cup bread crumbs
1 tablespoon butter
1 egg, beaten
½ cup celery, diced
½ cup onion, chopped
½ teaspoon salt
¼ teaspoon pepper

Preheat oven to 350 degrees. Grease a 2-quart baking dish.

Parboil eggplant in boiling water until tender, about 7 minutes. Drain. Combine eggplant with remaining ingredients and stir until well combined. Pour into prepared baking dish and bake for about 30 minutes.

Jo Anne Brown

SQUASH PUFFS

2 cups squash, cooked and mashed
1 egg, beaten
1 tablespoon melted butter
1 teaspoon salt
½ teaspoon sugar
¼ teaspoon cinnamon
¼ teaspoon pepper

Preheat oven to 400 degrees. Cut 3-inch rounds of parchment paper and place on oiled baking sheets.

In a large bowl, combine all ingredients and blend well. Put mixture in a pastry bag and pipe decorative mounds onto parchment paper. Bake for about 10 to 15 minutes or until nicely browned. Remove with spatula and slip off of the parchment paper.

Jo Anne Brown

ESCALLOPED CHEESE AND TOMATOES

2 cups tomatoes; peeled, seeded and
   chopped
2 cups bread crumbs
1 cup cheddar cheese, diced
½ cup celery, minced
¼ teaspoon salt
4 tablespoons butter

Preheat oven to 325 degrees. Butter a 2-quart baking dish.

In a large bowl, combine tomatoes, bread crumbs, cheese, celery and salt and toss until well mixed. Pour into prepared baking dish and dot with butter. Bake for 30 minutes.

Jo Anne Brown

IRISH COLCANNON

2 onions, chopped
⅔ cup milk
6 potatoes, cooked and mashed
4 tablespoons butter
Salt and pepper to taste
Minced parsley

Simmer onions in the milk until tender. Beat potatoes with onion and milk, butter, salt and pepper until light. Serve hot garnished with minced parsley.

Jo Anne Brown

RED CABBAGE AND APPLE

4 cups shredded red cabbage
2 tart apples, peeled and shredded
1 cup water
½ cup sugar
3 tablespoons lemon juice
1 teaspoon salt

Combine all ingredients in large sauce pan. Cover and simmer over low heat about 40 minutes, or until tender.

Mrs. Hattie L. Cresser

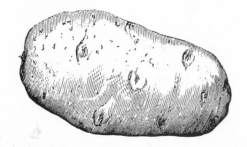

Potatoes for Each Day

Sunday - Mashed. Peel thin, steam, place in pan and mash, adding milk, butter and salt. Beat until light.
Monday - Baked in jackets.
Tuesday - Peel and bake with roast of beef.
Wednesday - Slice thin and put in cold water for half an hour. Place in an ordinary baking dish with salt, pepper and milk. Bake for an hour, remove and put butter on top.
Thursday - Peel and steam, and serve whole.
Friday - Cut in thin, long slices, sprinkle with salt and pepper, and fry in butter or beef drippings.
Saturday - Boil in the jackets.
Lillian L. Dickinson

Dry Corn

We always have this on Thanksgiving and Christmas in memory of the many Oregon Pioneers in our family.

Blanch fresh ears of corn for about 1 minute. Cut off kernels in two slices, rather than one deep slice to the cob. Put on baking sheet in one layer and dry in a very slow oven, stirring often. Store in a glass jar with a lid.

To sun dry, cover corn with cheesecloth and put on a shed roof in the sun. Bring into the house at night then put back in the sun every day until dry.

To cook, place corn and ham hock in a large pot and cover with water. Cook slowly for 2 to 3 hours, or until corn is tender.

Zelma Newman

CORN FRITTERS

2 cups grated corn
½ cup milk
1 egg, beaten
1 teaspoon melted butter
1 teaspoon salt
⅛ teaspoon pepper
2 cups flour
1 teaspoon baking powder
3 tablespoons oil

In a large bowl, combine corn, milk, egg, butter, salt and pepper and blend well. Stir in flour and baking powder until smooth. Heat oil in a large skillet over medium heat. Drop batter by the tablespoonful into hot oil and fry until golden on both sides. Drain on paper towels. Serve hot.

Jo Anne Brown

FARMER'S CORN PUDDING

2 cups grated corn
2 eggs, beaten
1½ tablespoons melted butter
½ cup green bell pepper, minced
2 cups scalded milk
Salt and pepper to taste

Preheat oven to 325 degrees. Butter a 2-quart baking dish.

In a large bowl, combine corn, eggs, butter and green pepper and stir until well combined. Pour in scalded milk gradually, stirring until well blended. Season with salt and pepper. Pour into prepared baking dish and bake for about 40 minutes, or until golden.

Jo Anne Brown

Roast Corn

Turn back husks and pick off the silk. Re-cover with the husks and roast in the hot ashes of a wood fire.
Clara Kaneaster

KRIS' GERMAN POTATO SALAD

6 medium potatoes
1 large onion, finely chopped
½ pound bacon, diced
½ cup bacon fat or oil
½ cup beef broth
½ cup cider vinegar
1½ teaspoons salt
1 teaspoon black pepper

Cook potatoes in their jackets, in simmering water until just tender. As soon as they are cool enough to handle, peel and dice. Put potatoes in a large bowl and add onions. Cook the bacon until crisp, reserve fat, and add bacon to potatoes. In a separate bowl, stir together the bacon fat, beef broth, vinegar, salt and pepper. Pour dressing over potatoes and toss well to mix. Serve warm.

Colby Lee Whipple

POTATO PANCAKES

4 medium potatoes, peeled
1 small onion, peeled
1 egg, beaten
3 tablespoons flour
2 tablespoons milk
½ teaspoon baking powder
½ teaspoon salt
¼ teaspoon pepper
Oil for frying

Grate potatoes and onion into a large bowl and let them sit in their own liquid for 10 minutes. Drain. Add remaining ingredients and blend well. Drop by spoonfuls onto hot, oiled griddle. Brown well on both sides. Serve with meat or fish, plain or with jelly.

Opal Schweiss
Betsy Krause

POTATO PATTIES

My grandmother, Josephine Jeaudoin, passed away in 1944 at the age of 89. She was associated with the Hudson Bay Company.

2 cups mashed potatoes
1 egg yolk, slightly beaten
2 tablespoons onion, finely minced
Salt and pepper to taste
Flour for dredging
Oil for frying

Combine potatoes, egg yolk, onion, salt and pepper and form into 6 patties. Dredge lightly in flour. Heat oil in large skillet over medium heat. Add the potato patties and cook until they have a brown-glazed crust on both sides. Serve hot.

Lewis Jeadoin

Dandelion Greens Wilted Salad

Pick very young dandelion greens. Wash thoroughly. Make a mixture of rendered bacon pieces, bacon fat, small amount of sugar, a little salt and several tablespoons of vinegar. Heat and serve immediately over greens.

Margaret Pauly Tate

DEPRESSION SAUSAGE

1 pound dried peas, black-eyed peas or
    whippoorwill peas
1 small onion, finely chopped
¼ cup flour
1 teaspoon sage
1 teaspoon salt
¼ teaspoon dried red pepper flakes
Bacon drippings for frying

Cook peas in 12 cups water until tender, about 1 hour. Drain and mash thoroughly. Stir in onion. Combine flour, sage, salt and red pepper flakes and beat into peas. Mixture will be stiff. Shape into a sausage and fry in the bacon drippings until browned on all sides.

Lois McClendon

MOTHER'S SALAD DRESSING

When mayonnaise was first used on potato salad, I thought it was terrible, we had to have the cooked dressing. Some of the commercial salads bought in grocery stores have a similar dressing, but not as good as this of course! Modern tastes welcome other seasonings—mustard, celery seed, etc.

2 eggs, well beaten
¾ cup sugar
⅔ cup vinegar
2 tablespoons butter

Combine ingredients in the top of a double boiler. Cook over simmering water, whisking constantly, until thick. Use to dress potato salad.
Variation: add ¾ cup cream to dress shredded cabbage.

Elna Elliott Schmidt

SPINACH SAUTÉED WITH BACON

2 slices bacon, finely chopped
2 tablespoons onion, minced
10 ounces fresh spinach, chopped
Salt and pepper to taste

In a frying pan, cook the bacon over medium heat until crisp. Remove all but 1 teaspoon bacon fat, add the onion and sauté until transparent. Add the spinach and sauté until cooked through, about 5 minutes. Season with salt and pepper. Serve immediately.

Leslie J. Whipple

STAY CRISP SALAD

8 cups cabbage, shredded
2 cups carrots, grated
½ cup onion, finely chopped
1 envelope unflavored gelatin
¼ cup cold water
1 cup vinegar
⅔ cup sugar
1½ teaspoons celery seed
1½ teaspoons black pepper

Combine cabbage, carrots, onion and ½ cup cold water. Chill at least 1 hour. Soften gelatin in ¼ cup cold water, set aside. In a small saucepan, stir together vinegar, sugar, celery seed and black pepper. Bring to a boil, stirring constantly, and whisk in gelatin. Remove from heat and cool. Drain vegetables and toss with the dressing. Serve with Mother's Oven Stew (page 50).

W. Freeman

Fish & Fowl

Christmas Dinner Menu
from Farm News, December 1909

Cream of Celery Soup
(Served with toast cut in narrow strips)
Cucumber Pickles   (home-made)
Roast Turkey (oyster dressing)
Mashed potatoes
Baked and buttered "sweets"
Cold slaw   Celery
Cranberry sauce (served cold)
Quince preserves   Applesauce (hot)
Pumpkin pie   American cheese
Canned peaches and cream
White cake
Coffee (piping hot)
Hickory nuts, walnuts, or butternuts
(cracked before serving)

Samuel Dement came to Oregon with his wife, Caroline, and son, Russell, in 1852. They settled in Coos County where descendants still live.

Helen B. Dement
(Mrs. Wallace B. Dement)

DAD'S OYSTER DRESSING

½ cup butter
6 stalks celery, chopped
2 large onions, chopped
3 to 4 bags (7½-ounce) Franz seasoned
     bread crumbs
2 tablespoons dry parsley
1½ tablespoons poultry seasoning
1 tablespoon salt
1 to 2 teaspoons black pepper
5 to 6 pints oysters with their liquid,
     chopped
3 eggs, lightly beaten
1 cup milk
2 to 3 bay leaves

Heat butter in a large frying pan over medium heat. Add celery and onions and sauté until soft. Place bread crumbs in a large bowl and stir in parsley, poultry seasoning, salt and pepper. Add sautéed vegetables and oysters. Mix the milk and eggs and add to the mixture. Toss to moisten and mix ingredients. Stuff the turkey, placing 1 bay leaf in the neck and 2 in the body. Bake remaining dressing in a covered baking dish for the last hour of roasting the turkey.

Stewart M. Whipple

Fried Spring Chicken Southern Style

1 chicken   1 cup lard
½ cup flour   Salt and pepper

Select a large, plump spring chicken. Kill, scald and pluck. Draw and cut into the natural joints. Then put them into ice water for five minutes. Drain and place on a platter for two hours. Dredge in flour and sprinkle with salt and pepper. Place the lard in a frying pan and when it is hot, sauté the chicken in it, taking care to turn often so it will not burn, but cook thoroughly. Serve with cream gravy.

Vera Merwin Schneider Botorf

CHICKEN CONTINENTAL

15 chicken thighs
1 cup flour
1 teaspoon salt
¾ pound butter
1 medium onion, finely chopped
1 pound mushrooms (optional)
½ cup dry sherry
8 chicken bullion cubes
¼ cup hot water
2 pounds sour cream

Skin and bone chicken thighs and cut into 1½-inch pieces. Combine flour and salt then dredge chicken pieces in the flour mixture, shaking off excess. Heat 6 tablespoons of the butter in a large skillet over medium heat. When hot, add as many chicken pieces that will fit in the skillet without crowding, and sauté until golden brown on all sides. Remove with a slotted spoon and put in a large pot. Add more butter to skillet and repeat until all chicken is sautéed. Add more butter to the skillet and sauté onion until translucent and add to pot. Sauté mushrooms and add to pot if desired. Pour sherry into skillet, and cook for 2 minutes, scraping up all browned bits. Pour into pot. Dissolve chicken bullion cubes in the hot water and add to pot. Stir in sour cream. Cover pot and simmer gently over low heat for 50 to 60 minutes. Serve over white rice.

Jerry Crowley

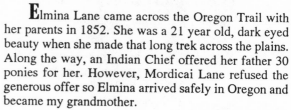

Elmina Lane came across the Oregon Trail with her parents in 1852. She was a 21 year old, dark eyed beauty when she made that long trek across the plains. Along the way, an Indian Chief offered her father 30 ponies for her. However, Mordicai Lane refused the generous offer so Elmina arrived safely in Oregon and became my grandmother.

Mary Bryant Hodge
Frances Bryant Thies

BAKED SALMON WITH WILD MUSHROOMS

1 pound salmon filet
½ teaspoon salt
3 ounces fresh wild mushrooms such as
    chanterelles, boletus, morels
    or shiitake, thinly sliced
1 tablespoon butter
1 tablespoon fresh lemon juice
1 tablespoon fresh chives, minced

Preheat oven to 350 degrees.
Place the fish, skin side down, in a shallow baking dish. Season with the salt. Place the mushrooms on the salmon and dot with butter. Sprinkle lemon juice and chives over all. Bake for 20 minutes.

Leslie J. Whipple

BEST PAN FRIED FISH

1 pound fish fillets
½ cup yellow cornmeal
½ cup flour
½ teaspoon salt
½ teaspoon dill, (optional)
⅛ teaspoon black pepper
1 egg, beaten
2 tablespoons water
2 tablespoons butter or margarine
2 tablespoons oil

Combine cornmeal, flour, salt, dill and pepper in a shallow dish. Combine egg and water in another shallow dish. Dip fish fillets in dry mixture; then in egg mixture; then again in dry mixture. Heat butter and oil in large skillet. Cook fish over medium heat until it flakes easily.

Josephine Koontz

MINNIE IDA'S RAZOR CLAM TIMBALES

3½ cups finely minced razor clams
⅔ cup fresh bread crumbs
4 eggs, separated
1 tablespoon melted butter
½ teaspoon salt
¼ teaspoon black pepper
⅛ teaspoon cayenne pepper

Preheat oven to 350 degrees. Butter an 8-inch ring mold.

In a large bowl, combine clams, bread crumbs and egg yolks and let sit for 10 minutes. Stir in butter, salt, pepper and cayenne. Beat egg whites until stiff and fold into clam mixture. Pour mixture into prepared mold and set in a larger pan filled with enough water to come halfway up the sides of the mold. Bake for about 30 minutes, or until knife inserted in the center comes out clean.

Gerald W. Frank

Food to the Indian was more than physical nourishment, it was spiritual nourishment as well. In this cultural area we call the Northwest Coast, we had immense respect for the great resources that the Creator had provided for us. The great salmon runs were highly regarded, and the salmon were considered scouts from an honored nation. The first salmon caught was honored with a feast. At the feasts, salmon were ceremonially prepared by women with the finest reputations, songs were sung and everyone received a piece of the fish. It was like a sacrament. The Indians believed this respect would ensure that the salmon would not be offended in any way and would guarantee good salmon runs for the future. In the minds of the Indians, the salmon are linked with immortality, sustenance, continuance and rebirth. The salmon do not merely run in the rivers and the oceans, they run in our blood.

Chief Don Lelooska.

In 1852 my great-grandfather, William S. Wilson, and his wife, May Anne McNutt Wilson, started across the plains to Oregon. Passing through the identical spot on which Boise, Idaho is located, Mr. Wilson's party met an emigrant train on the verge of starvation. Their supplies were completely gone, they had only rifles and could not find any game. The Wilson party was also low, but Mr. Wilson had a shotgun. With this he shot a sackful of jack rabbits, which furnished the principal food for the party for some days. The two parties kept together until a settler's store was reached.

D. W. Wilson

SALMON LOAF

My great-great-grandparents, Johan and Otilla Berthold, came to Oregon in 1844. Their daughter, Mary, was two years old at the time and a son, Phillip, was born in December of 1844 after crossing the plains. Johan was killed and scalped by Indians in the gold fields of Northern California.

2 eggs, beaten
2 cups bread crumbs
2 cups cooked salmon
½ cup mayonnaise
½ cup celery, finely diced
½ cup onion, minced
1 teaspoon lemon juice
1 10-ounce can cream
    of mushroom soup
Salt and pepper to taste

Preheat oven to 350 degrees. Grease a 9x5x3-inch loaf pan.

Combine all ingredients and blend well. Put into prepared pan and bake for about 1 hour.

Virginia Brayler

LOBSTER CROQUETTES

2 tablespoons butter
3 tablespoons flour
1 cup milk
2 cups lobster meat, chopped
1 teaspoon parsley, minced
1 teaspoon lemon juice
½ teaspoon salt
¼ teaspoon pepper
2 eggs, lightly beaten
2 cups bread crumbs
Oil for frying

In a heavy sauce pan, melt butter over medium heat. Stir in flour, and cook, stirring constantly for about 2 minutes. Pour in milk slowly, stirring constantly until sauce thickens. Remove from heat and set aside to cool. In a large bowl, combine cooled white sauce, lobster, parsley, lemon juice, salt and pepper and stir until well blended. Shape into 8 croquettes. Dip in beaten egg then coat with bread crumbs. Heat 3-inches of oil to 375 degrees. Add a few croquettes at a time, do not crowd, and brown well on all sides. Drain on paper towels. Serve with Tartar Sauce.

Tartar Sauce
    1 cup mayonnaise
    1 tablespoon capers, minced
    1 tablespoon dill pickle, minced
    1 tablespoon olives, minced
    ½ teaspoon parsley. minced
    ½ teaspoon onion, grated

Fold all ingredients together and chill.

Mrs. Hattie L. Cresser

Grandma's Chicken and Noodles

This recipe has been passed down through our family from pioneer ancestors who came to Oregon by wagon train.

Chicken Broth:
Kill and gut one fat hen. Behead and dip in scalding water. Pluck clean. Boil chicken in enough water to cover, with ¼ teaspoon salt, until meat falls away from the bones. Save broth. Remove chicken from bones. Discard bones in a safe place away from dogs and cats.

Noodles:
Break six eggs into a large bowl. Beat until blended. Add flour and ¼ teaspoon salt gradually, until mixture is thick enough to roll. Flour board and roll dough thin. Let sit for as long as possible. With knife cut dough into narrow strips.

In large pan heat broth to a boil. Return chicken pieces to pan. Heat to boil. Add noodles one at a time, stirring. Simmer until noodles are desired tenderness, stirring occasionally. If broth is not thick enough, mix flour and water to paste and stir into simmering broth until desired thickness.

Serves six light eaters, four hearty.

Kay Hanville

CLAMS NEWBURG

2 tablespoons butter
1 cup cream
2 cups cooked, minced clams
½ cup sherry
1 teaspoon paprika
½ teaspoon salt
2 egg yolks
Toast points

Melt butter in the top of a double boiler. Stir in cream and heat through but do not let boil. Add clams, sherry, paprika and salt and heat over barely simmering water. Stir some of the cream mixture into the egg yolks, then whisk into the cream mixture. Whisk constantly until thickened. Serve over toast points.

Mrs. Hattie L. Cresser

SALMON PATTIES

2 cups cooked salmon
2 cups bread crumbs
1 small onion, finely chopped
2 tablespoons green bell pepper, minced
2 eggs, lightly beaten
2 tablespoons oil
Salt and pepper to taste

Preheat oven to 350 degrees. Lightly oil a muffin pan.

In a large bowl, combine all ingredients and mix well. Spoon into prepared muffin pan and bake for about 30 minutes.

Jo Anne Brown

Pan Fried Pheasant

Clean and cut up pheasant. Roll in flour seasoned with salt, pepper and garlic salt, if desired. Using fat or shortening, pan fry until brown and tender.

Gail E. Orell
Hersey House
Ashland, Oregon

CRABMEAT CASSEROLE

2 cups flaked crabmeat
¾ cup ground almonds
1 teaspoon onion juice
1 teaspoon Worcestershire
    sauce
⅛ teaspoon salt
1 egg, separated
1 cup heavy cream

Preheat oven to 300 degrees. Grease a 2-quart mold.

In a large bowl, combine crab, almonds, onion juice, Worcestershire sauce, salt and egg yolk and blend well. Beat egg white until stiff and fold into mixture. Beat cream until soft peaks then carefully fold into mixture. Pour into prepared mold and set into a larger pan filled with enough water to come halfway up sides of the mold. Bake for about 40 minutes, or until center is set.

Jo Anne Brown

OYSTERS À LA POULETTE

½ cup butter
1 small onion, grated
3 tablespoons flour
2 cups chicken broth
3 egg yolks, beaten
3 pints oysters
Toast as an accompaniment

In a large sauce pan, melt butter over medium heat. Add onions and sauté until soft but not brown. Whisk in flour and cook until mixture thickens slightly. Whisk in chicken broth in a thin stream, and cook until slightly thickened. Reduce heat to low and whisk in egg yolks. Do not let boil. Stir in oysters and simmer gently until cooked through. Serve on toast or in ramekins.

Gerald W. Frank

CREAMED CHICKEN

We had a houseful after church on Sundays. My folks were farmers and no one they met were strangers, they always invited friends over for a good country dinner.

1 stewing hen, cut up
1 tablespoon cornstarch
Salt and pepper to taste

Place chicken in a large pot and cover with water. Simmer about 2 hours or until meat falls off the bone. Strain the stock and return to the pot. Discard bones and cut meat into bite-sized pieces, set aside. Combine cornstarch with 1 tablespoon cold water. Bring stock to a boil and whisk in cornstarch mixture. Stir meat into thickened stock and heat through. Season with salt and pepper.

Serve over Baking Powder Biscuits (page 3).

Janice M. Hardy

BAKED HALIBUT WITH CHEESE

4 halibut steaks
½ teaspoon salt
½ teaspoon paprika
½ cup bread crumbs
½ cup Parmesan cheese, grated
1 tablespoon butter

Preheat oven to 325 degrees. Grease a baking pan.

Place halibut in prepared pan and sprinkle with salt and paprika. Bake for 15 minutes. Mix bread crumbs and Parmesan together. Remove halibut from oven and spread with bread crumb mixture. Dot with butter. Return to oven and bake an additional 15 minutes or until cooked.

Dagmar Skulason Fisher

Meats & Game

EASTER BREAKFAST

In the 1920s we would hike up the hill to attend the Easter Sunrise Service at Washington Park in Portland, Oregon. This certainly hit the spot upon our return!

    1 cup lean ham, ground
    2½ tablespoons flour
    2 cups milk
    4 eggs
    Salt and pepper to taste
    4 slices toast

Lightly brown ham in a large skillet. Stir in flour and mix well. Pour in milk gradually and stir until thickened. Break each egg, one by one, carefully into a different place in the skillet. Spoon the simmering gravy over the eggs for 2 to 3 minutes, or until they are set. Season with salt and pepper. Serve over toast for breakfast or mashed potatoes for dinner.

Jean W. Cusick

SWEDISH MEATBALLS

    1 cup bread crumbs
    1 cup whipping cream
    ½ pound ground beef
    ¼ pound ground veal
    ¼ pound ground pork
    2 eggs, beaten
    2 tablespoons onion, minced
    2 teaspoons salt
    ¼ teaspoon pepper
    ¼ teaspoon allspice
    4 tablespoons butter
    Mashed potatoes as an accompaniment

In a large bowl, combine bread crumbs and cream and let sit for 10 minutes. Add beef, veal pork, eggs, onion, salt, pepper and allspice and mix until well blended. Shape into 2-inch meatballs. Heat butter in a large skillet over medium heat, then cook meatballs until well browned on all sides and cooked through. Serve with mashed potatoes.

Ruth Lillian Hovey Johnson

Baked Squirrel

Skin squirrel and gut. Soak cut-up squirrel in salt water overnight. In the morning, drain, wipe dry and dip in flour seasoned with salt, pepper and a little garlic salt. Brown in 3 tablespoons of fat or shortening. Drain off fat. Add 1 cup water and bay leaves; cover and bake at 350 degrees for 1 to 1½ hours, or until tender. This is best done in a Dutch oven, and can be cooked over an open campfire.

Gail E. Orell
Hersey House
Ashland, Oregon

SOLOMI
(BEEF OR VENISON)

5 pounds lean, ground beef; or 4 pounds
venison plus 1 pound pork,
ground together
6 teaspoons Morton's Tender Quick salt
2½ teaspoons black pepper
2½ teaspoons mustard seed
2½ teaspoons garlic salt
1 teaspoon liquid smoke flavoring

Mix all ingredients together in a large bowl and
refrigerate for four days. Stir well each day. On the
fourth day, roll mixture into 5 sausage shapes approximately 12-inches long and 1½-inches round.
Place on a rack in the oven over a pan to catch the
drippings. Bake at 150 degrees for about 8 hours,
turning every 2 hours.

Virginia M. Nelson

BARBECUE BEEF SLOPPY JOES

1 1½ to 2 pounds chuck roast
2 medium onions, diced
2 tablespoons lard
2 tablespoons Worcestershire sauce
¾ cup catsup
¾ cup beef broth
3 tablespoons vinegar
¼ teaspoon pepper
1 teaspoon chili powder
1 teaspoon paprika
1 teaspoon salt

Cook chuck roast until medium done. Sauté
onions in lard until lightly browned. Add all remaining ingredients and let simmer for about 20
minutes. Grind cooked meat in a meat grinder using
large-coarse blade. Pour sauce mixture over ground
meat and mix well.

NOTE: The flavor gets better 2 to 3 days after
preparing this barbecue sauce. Also freezes well.

Helen Hall

Sarah Smith's Meat Pies

Sarah Smith was the wife of Asa Bowen Smith, a
missionary associate of Dr. Whitman. They crossed the
country in 1838. Sarah tells about making meat pies
along the trail and how she improvised to make up for
the lack of a rolling pin and bread board. The group of
missionaries Sarah was traveling with was lucky
enough to have brought a reflector oven with them
which made baking much easier. Sarah writes, "Spent
this morning sewing a hunter's dress and this afternoon
made a couple of pies, chopped meat with a butcher
knife on the bark of a cottonwood tree which Mr. S
peeled off. Rolled the crust with a crooked stick in a
hollow bark, baked them in the tin baker out of doors
in the wind but they were good and we have had a good
supper."

1 pound ground beef
Salt and pepper
Pastry enough for a 2-crust pie

Preheat oven to 350 degrees.
Cook ground beef, breaking apart as it cooks, until
it loses its red color. Season with salt and pepper to
taste.
Divide pastry into two pieces. On a lightly floured
board, roll out each piece to about 10-inch circles. Place
on a baking sheet. Spoon half of the meat onto each
pastry circle, placing it on one-half of the dough, and
leaving a 1-inch border. Moisten edges of dough and
fold the dough over the filling. Press edges together to
seal. Cut 4 slits on top to allow steam to escape. Repeat
with other pastry circle. Bake for about 20 minutes, or
until nicely browned.

June Cummins
Park Ranger
Whitman Mission National Historic Site

A GOOD CAMP DISH

My mother cooked on a wood stove. If the oven got too hot while she was baking, she would prop it open with a stick of stove wood until it cooled. If she couldn't get it hot fast enough for frying or boiling, Mother took the lid off the stove and placed the kettle directly on the fire.

> 1 pound bacon
> 1 can corn
> 2 eggs
> Salt and pepper

Dice bacon and fry until crisp. Drain off all but 2 tablespoons of bacon fat. Add corn. When hot, add eggs and stir briskly until cooked. Season to taste.

Louise Schreiner

Sarah Smith's Buffalo Gravy

The following method of cooking the ever present buffalo was a favorite, and offered a change from the usual roasting, boiling or frying. Sarah Smith makes this entry in her diary, "Have just taken our supper of buffalo. We love it very much when it is cooked good as it was tonight. Mr. Gray and Mr. Smith are cooks. They sometimes boil and fry, sometimes chop it and make it appear like sausage. After it is fried, make a milk gravy and it is very fine. Such was our supper tonight. We eat no bread at all, are saving the flour, fearing we shall need it when on the sandy plain there is no game."

> 1 pound ground beef
> Salt and pepper to taste
> 4 tablespoons flour
> 2 cups milk

In a heavy skillet, brown the ground beef, stirring to break up chunks, until it loses its red color. Season with salt and pepper. Stir in the flour. Pour in the milk slowly, stirring constantly. Cook until thickened. Adjust the seasoning. Serve over hot biscuits, toast or baked or mashed potatoes.

June Cummins
Park Ranger
Whitman Mission National Historic Site

GLAZE FOR BAKED HAM

My parents, Frank and Minnie Crouch, came to Oregon in 1909 and settled in Alameda. My father had invested their life savings in a copper mine. He worked in the mine and my mother ran the cookhouse for the mine crew.

Glaze:

> 4 cups red wine
> 2 cups honey
> 1 cup prepared mustard
> 1 bay leaf
> 1 teaspoon whole peppercorns
> 1 teaspoon whole cloves

Combine wine, honey, mustard, bay leaf, peppercorns and cloves in a saucepan and bring to a boil. Reduce heat to medium-low and simmer for 30 minutes. Baste ham with glaze often while baking.

Mrs. Rosalthe V. Dallas

Venison Steak

Pat ½-inch thick venison steak in seasoned flour. Pan fry in hot shortening, on medium-high heat. When done to desired color, place on plate and keep warm in oven. Add 2 tablespoons flour to the drippings. Stir in 1 cup milk, stirring continuously to avoid lumps. Ready when milk boils and the gravy is the desired thickness.

Gail E. Orell
Hersey House
Ashland, Oregon

CHEDDAR SWISS STEAK

My grandfather, Isaiah "Pony" Hall, came across the plains as a nine year old "bound boy". He ran away after years of being mistreated. Later, as an adult he drove freight wagons from The Dalles, Oregon to Boise, Idaho. He was nicknamed "Pony" because of his small size. He was five feet tall and drove several teams of horses hitched together.

2 tablespoons oil
¼ cup flour
1 teaspoon salt
¼ teaspoon black pepper
3 pounds round steak, about 2-inches
     thick
2 large onions, sliced
½ cup water
½ cup sour cream
½ cup cheddar cheese, shredded
¾ teaspoon paprika

Heat oil in a large, heavy skillet. Combine flour, salt and pepper, and dredge meat. Shake off excess and brown in hot oil on both sides. Sprinkle onions over meat. Combine remaining ingredients and pour over meat. Reduce heat to medium-low, cover and braise for about 1 hour, or until tender.

Almyra M. Walter

Pickled Meat

The following recipe was used to prepare the meat for my great-great-grandparents' Oregon Trail journey in the spring of 1852. Samuel Cresswell Braden and his wife Susannah Crobarger Braden left Missouri and arrived in the Umpqua Valley, Oregon in the fall.
For 100 pounds of meat:

8 pounds of salt
4½ gallons water
10 pounds of brown sugar
1 pound of saltpeter
4 tablespoonsful baking soda

To prepare the meat for pickling, let it lay in salt overnight or about 24 hours, then soak in fresh water 24 hours, which draws out all the blood. Place in keg or jar and pour the above pickling over the meat. Keep under a weight. If the pickling should become thickened pour off and boil again and pour over meat when it is thoroughly cold. To prepare the pickling, put water in a boiler with the salt, sugar and saltpeter and let boil, stirring often to keep the ingredients from burning to bottom of boiler. After it is boiling put soda in and skim off all skum from the liquid. Let stand overnight or thoroughly cool before using.

Mrs. Robert W. Cartwright

My great-grandfather, Reuben Lewis, came to Oregon in 1843 with the Elijah White immigration. He once killed eleven buffalo in one day, supplying meat for the whole company. He was one of the 52 men who founded the Provisional Government at Champoeg, Oregon.

Lucile Lewis Mills

CORNED VENISON OR BEEF

My great-grandparents, James and Eveline Officer came to Oregon in 1845 over the Oregon Trail. They left Missouri with eight children and arrived with nine, a daughter was born enroute. They came in four wagons with 22 oxen, 20 head of cattle and 3 mules. Provisions were: 400 pounds of meal, 1800 pounds of flour, 680 pounds of bacon, 45 pounds of lead, 25 pounds of gun powder and 9 guns and pistols. They were among the group traveling the "Meek Cut-off", the wagon train now famous for discovering the "Blue Bucket" gold mine. The location of the gold discovery was lost and searchers still have not been able to pinpoint the site.

6 pounds venison or beef brisket
4 quarts hot water
1 cup coarse salt
2½ tablespoons pickling spice
1 tablespoon brown sugar
2 cloves garlic, crushed
¼ teaspoon saltpeter

Place meat in a deep, stainless steel or other non reactive pot or a large ceramic crock. Combine remaining ingredients together and pour over meat. Place a weight on the meat to keep it submerged, and cover pot. Refrigerate for 7 days, turning meat every 2 days.

To cook, cover meat with fresh water and bring to a boil. Reduce heat to low, cover pot and simmer until done, about 1 hour per pound of meat.

Roberta Seeber

My grandfather, John Cole and his family, left Missouri April 15, 1852 and were six months crossing the plains by ox team. They settled with other pioneers near Cottage Grove, Oregon, known at that time as Slab Town. My grandfather took a Donation Land Claim and built a log cabin and lived in that until 1863 when he built a house of lumber.

I was eleven years old before I saw a heating stove. All the houses had open fireplaces. Some didn't have cook stoves but did all their cooking in the fireplace. There was an iron bar across the fireplace with a hook on it, and they hung their iron kettles on this hook above the fire and cooked their beans and boiled their meat. They baked their bread in a Dutch oven by setting the oven-kettle on a few live coals, and put more live coals on the lid. Bread baked this way was very good.

We had no white sugar, but bought brown sugar by the barrel. My grandfather hauled his wheat to the flour mill in the fall of the year and had enough wheat ground to last us a year. He butchered from ten to twelve hogs each fall. Every settler had a smokehouse to smoke their meat in. The smokehouse had a dirt floor. After the meat was salted down for a length of time, it was hung on spikes, and a small fire was built under the meat. They used vine maple wood to smoke their meat. They bought green coffee in the bulk, then roasted it in bake pans in the oven. Then ground it in a coffee mill attached to the wall in the kitchen.

Anna M. (Cole) Land
Opal Land Eversole

Salt Pork and Fried Apples

This was a dish actually made on the wagon train. My grandmother Ballinger remembered her mother making this dish as they came West to Oregon Country.

Cut half a pound of salt pork in slices. Fry slowly in a deep frying pan. When done, take up on a hot dish. Meanwhile, wash, wipe and cut in slices 6 sour apples. When the pork is taken up, put apples into frying pan and cook in the gravy until tender. Serve hot on the platter with the pork.

Marcia Gray

MEATLOAF

1 pound ground beef
1 pound bulk sausage
1 egg, slightly beaten
12 saltine crackers, crushed medium fine
1½ cups milk
Salt and pepper to taste

Preheat oven to 350 degrees. Grease a 9x5x3-inch loaf pan.

Combine ground beef, sausage and egg. Soak crackers in milk until soft then add to meat mixture. Season with salt and pepper. Bake about 45 minutes.

**Araminta Phillips
Daraleen Wade**

Bison Jerky

Slice bison meat along the grain into strips ⅛-inch thick, ½-inch wide, and 2 to 3 inches long. Hang them on a rack in a pan and bake at 200 degrees to dry. To prepare outside, suspend them over a fire or drape them on bushes to dry in the sun.

Lynda Hatch

SAUSAGE AND EGG BAKE

1 pound bulk sausage
12 slices bread
Butter, softened
2 cups cheese, shredded
3 cups milk
4 eggs
Salt and pepper to taste

Preheat oven to 325 degrees. Butter a 2-quart baking dish.

In a skillet, brown sausage until crumbly, drain. Trim crusts from bread and spread lightly with butter. Layer bread, sausage and cheese in baking dish. Blend milk, eggs, salt and pepper until smooth. Pour over ingredients in baking dish and refrigerate overnight. Bake for about 1 hour, or until the custard is set.

Josephine Koontz

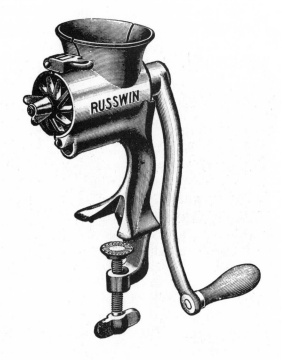

POT ROAST OF BEEF

3 pounds beef rump roast
Oil for browning
5 medium carrots, peeled and cut
    into 3-inch pieces
4 stalks celery, cut into 2-inch pieces
1 cup mushrooms, halved
½ cup onion, chopped
1 clove garlic, minced
1 cup beef consommé
1 cup sour cream
½ cup dry red wine
2 teaspoons salt
½ teaspoon paprika
¼ teaspoon black pepper
¼ cup flour

Heat oil in a heavy pot or Dutch oven. Brown beef on all sides. Add to the pot carrots, celery, mushrooms, onion, garlic, beef consommé, sour cream, red wine, salt, paprika and black pepper. Cover and simmer over low heat for about 2 hours.

To make venison tender and flavorful, braise in coffee. Use enough brewed coffee to fill the Dutch oven by 1-inch. Add meat, season with salt and pepper, then cover tightly and cook over low heat until meat is very tender.

Harlow Friday

Strain 2 cups of juice into a saucepan, add water to make 2 cups if necessary, and bring to a simmer. Whisk ¼ cup of juice into the flour until smooth, then whisk into juice in saucepan. Cook over medium heat, stirring constantly, until gravy is thickened. Serve over Pot Roast.

Elizabeth Frericks

My great-great-grandfather James Watt, his wife Mary Scott Watt and their son Ahio Scott Watt came to Oregon from St. Louis in 1848. Ahio met Mary Elder, who was on the wagon train with her father, and they married shortly after they arrived in Oregon. This is the story of how Ahio and Mary met:

We have been heading toward The Promised Land for three weeks already, and I have decided to keep some notes as we go. Oregon, here we come.

My name is Ahio Scott Watt. I am nineteen years of age, and am traveling in a party with my folks, John and Mary Watt. My brother John will meet us in Oregon. He is an Army scout.

It has been raining for a week now, which makes for slow going. Mr. Elder's flock of sheep all look like mud balls with feet. We are all down in the dumps. Mary Elder manages to keep her smile though, and is always glad to see me.

The rain finally quit last night, and there will be a general meeting this evening.

There was much talk at the fire last night. Some of the men want to go to California now, Pa said that as far as he knew, there was nothing in California worth the trip. Oregon has so much more to offer anyone who would work for it. Farther along the Trail, some of the wagons will split off and head south.

The women cooked up a real good feed after the meeting. We had buffalo stew, and I got a couple of chunks of the hump. It was good. There ain't much in the way of green, but the women did pretty well with what they could find along the way. Wild onions sure helped the stew.

I ate with Mary, she is such pleasant company. Her family comes from Illinois, and her father knows Abraham Lincoln, the politician.

Pa and Mr. Peck and I were out hunting all day. We spotted a bunch of antelope, and managed to get close enough to kill four. We also got a mess of prairie chickens. It looks like good eating for a while.

This morning we had services and buried three people, the Smiths and young Hal Emery. They had been down with the croup. All good folks, and we'll miss them.

The weather has been hot and dry. We can see clouds over the prairie ahead, but no rain. Dust covers everything. I have to keep a bandanna over my mouth and nose while we're moving, and the food still tastes like grit.

Today we all worked at separating those who were breaking off for California from the rest. I'll truly miss some of the friends I've made. Mary and her folks will go on to Oregon with the bigger party.

I have decided to get up enough nerve to ask Mr. Elder's permission to walk out with Mary. I think she likes me and I know how I feel about her. . . . .

Henry James Jackson II (Hank)

MOTHER'S OVEN STEW

This is a recipe I remember from early childhood. Mother served it with homemade bread and Stay Crisp Salad (page 30).

2 pounds stew meat; elk, venison or beef,
   cut into 2 inch pieces
4 cups potatoes, cut into 2 inch pieces
4 cups carrots, cut into 2 inch pieces
2 cups celery, cut into 2 inch pieces
2 cups turnips, cut into 2 inch pieces
1 cup onion, cut into 2 inch pieces
4 cups canned tomatoes
1 tablespoon sugar
2 teaspoons salt
1 teaspoon black pepper
1 teaspoon nutmeg
1 cup water

Preheat oven to 250 degrees.

In a large Dutch oven or oven-proof pot, combine meat, potatoes, carrots, celery, turnips, onion and tomatoes. Combine sugar, salt, black pepper, nutmeg and water together. Stir until sugar and salt dissolve then pour over other ingredients. Cover and bake 4 hours.

W. Freeman

Head Cheese

Clean a pig's head thoroughly, removing eyes, and ears and cut off snout. Remove all blood clots. Cover with water and boil until meat falls from bones. Remove meat from bones and separate meat coarsely. Thicken the stock with a little cornmeal, not too thick. Add salt, pepper and sage to taste. Place in molds to cool.

Louise Schreiner

STANDARD BEEF HASH

2 tablespoons shortening
1½ cups onion, chopped
3 cups cooked beef, coarsely ground
3 cups potatoes, finely diced
1 cup beef stock or gravy
1 teaspoon salt
¼ teaspoon black pepper

Melt shortening in a large frying pan. Add onion and sauté until soft, but not brown. Stir in remaining ingredients, cover and cook over medium-low heat until potatoes are cooked, about 20 minutes. Uncover and brown lightly, stirring occasionally.

Elizabeth Frericks

FRIED PIGS FEET

6 pigs' feet
Juice of 1 lemon
1 cup flour
¾ teaspoon baking powder
½ teaspoon salt
¼ teaspoon pepper
2 eggs, beaten
½ cup milk
Oil or lard for deep frying

Wash pigs' feet well, then place in a large pot and cover with cold water and lemon juice. Bring to a boil, then reduce heat to low and simmer until very tender, about 3 hours. Remove from broth and allow to cool completely.

In a shallow dish, sift flour, baking powder, salt and pepper. Add eggs and milk and whisk until smooth. Split pigs' feet in half with a sharp knife. Dip in batter and fry in deep fat heated to 365 degrees until golden brown on all sides. Drain on paper towels and serve very hot.

Mrs. Opal A. Eversole

Bison Steak

Render some fat in a hot skillet. Add sirloin of bisonsteak and sear on both sides. At lower heat, cook as beefsteak until done. For gravy, add a tablespoon of flour to the pan drippings and cook until brown. Stirring constantly, add a cup of milk and bring to a boil. Salt to taste.

Lynda Hatch

BEEF STROGANOFF FAMILY STYLE

1½ pounds sirloin steak, cut into
    ½ inch cubes
½ teaspoon salt
½ teaspoon paprika
⅛ teaspoon pepper
⅛ teaspoon garlic salt
¼ cup butter
1 medium onion, coarsely chopped
1 cup beef bouillon or beef broth
1 teaspoon Worcestershire sauce
2 cups sour cream

Season sirloin cubes with salt, paprika, pepper and garlic salt. Heat all but 1 tablespoon of the butter in a large skillet over medium heat. Add beef to skillet and brown well on all sides. Remove the beef and set aside. Add remaining butter and onion to skillet and cook until transparent. Return beef and any accumulated juices to the pan. Add bouillon and Worcestershire sauce, reduce heat to medium-low and simmer for 15 minutes. Stir in sour cream and heat through but do not let boil or sauce will curdle. Serve over rice.

Mrs. Jacquie Young

WISCONSIN BRATWURST

10 pounds pork shoulder, ground
¼ cup salt
3 tablespoons white pepper, ground
2 tablespoons coriander, ground
1 tablespoon mace, ground
1½ teaspoons allspice, ground
1½ teaspoons cardamom, ground
1½ teaspoons celery seed
1½ teaspoons thyme, ground
Sausage casings

Combine all ingredients and mix together very well. Fill the sausage casings, twisting every 6 to 8 inches. Do not fill the casings too tightly or they will burst when cooked. Refrigerate for 2 days before using to allow the flavors to mature. Prick sausages all over with a needle before cooking. Bratwurst may be fried, grilled or poached. Sausages may be smoked.

Johan Mathiesen

Cakes

The Ridders Picnic was the big event of the year in the Wells and Suver, Oregon area. Merry-go-rounds, home-made ice cream stands and races made for a gay occasion. I remember that we always had Fried Chicken and Walnut Cake with Boiled Icing.

Beatrice Paget

MRS. FRIEDLANDER'S WALNUT CAKE

1 cup butter
2 cups sugar
4 eggs, separated
1 whole egg
1 cup milk
3 cups flour
3 teaspoons baking powder
1 cup walnuts, chopped
1 cup raisins, optional

Preheat oven to 350 degrees. Grease two 9-inch round cake pans.

In a large bowl, cream the butter well. Add sugar and cream until very light. Add 4 egg yolks and 1 whole egg and beat until smooth. Sift together flour and baking powder, then add alternately with milk, beating well after each addition. Beat the 4 egg whites until stiff then fold into batter. Gently fold in walnuts and raisins. Pour into prepared pans and bake 30 to 40 minutes, or until toothpick inserted in the center comes out clean. When cool, fill and frost with Boiled Icing.

Gerald W. Frank

BOILED ICING

1 cup sugar
¼ cup water
1 egg white
1 teaspoon vanilla

Boil the sugar and water together until it reaches the soft-ball stage, 234 degrees. Beat the egg white until stiff, then, beating constantly, pour the hot syrup in a thin stream into the egg white. Beat in vanilla and continue beating until cool and fluffy.

Gerald W. Frank

MRS. JAMES W. COOK'S BLACKBERRY CAKE

This is from my great-grandmother's cookbook from 1896. My great-grandfather, James W. Cook, and his brother were prominent businessmen in Portland. They owned the J.W. & V. Cook Salmon Packing Co. on the Oregon side of the Columbia River, since 1870.

⅔ cup butter
1 cup sugar
4 eggs
4 tablespoons sour milk
1 teaspoon baking soda
1 cup blackberries (wild berries preferred)
1½ cups flour

Cream the butter and sugar, add the eggs well beaten, the milk and soda, then the berries and lastly the flour. Bake in a loaf 40 minutes in a moderate oven and ice with boiled frosting.

Emily Crumpacker

PRIZE WINNING APPLESAUCE CAKE

1½ cups applesauce
1 cup sugar
½ cup butter
1½ cups flour
2 tablespoons cocoa powder
2 teaspoons baking soda
1 teaspoon cinnamon
¼ teaspoon cloves
¼ teaspoon nutmeg
1 cup raisins

Preheat oven to 350 degrees. Grease an 8-inch square cake pan.

In a large sauce pan, combine applesauce, sugar and butter. Warm over low heat just until butter melts. Remove from heat and add remaining ingredients. Beat until smooth. Pour batter into prepared pan and bake for about 25 to 30 minutes, or until toothpick inserted in the center comes out clean. May be iced with chocolate icing or vanilla cream cheese icing.

Marge Mayes

PIG PEN CAKE FROM 1880

3 cups sugar
¾ cup butter
3 eggs
¾ cup milk
1 teaspoon vanilla
3½ cups flour
2 teaspoons baking powder
1 teaspoon salt
Icing
Small colored candies or chopped nuts
        or raisins

Preheat oven to 350 degrees.

Cream the sugar and butter in a large bowl. Add the eggs and beat until smooth. Stir in the milk and vanilla. Sift together the flour, baking powder and salt and stir into the sugar mixture. Dough should be stiff like a cookie dough. Chill dough to make it easier to handle. Roll out dough on lightly floured board to ½-inch thickness. Cut into strips 1-inch wide, and 6-inches long. Place on ungreased cookie sheets and bake for about 12 to 15 minutes, or until golden. Cool on a rack.

Icing
1 egg white
1 cup powdered sugar

Beat egg white until foamy then beat in sugar.

To assemble: spread icing on cookie strips then stack like a pig pen. Put colored candies, nuts or raisins inside.

Lois McClendon

ORANGE CAKE

My great-great-grandfather, Thomas Manley Ramsdell, was the cattle driver on the second great wagon train in 1844.

> 2 cups sugar
> ½ cup butter
> 5 egg yolks, beaten
> Juice and zest of 1 large orange
> 2½ cups flour
> 2 teaspoons baking powder
> 3 egg whites

Preheat oven to 350 degrees. Butter and flour two 9-inch cake pans.

In a large bowl, cream the sugar and butter until light and fluffy. Add the egg yolks and the orange juice and zest and beat well. Sift the flour and baking powder together, then add to first mixture and blend until smooth. Beat egg whites until stiff then fold into batter. Pour batter into prepared pans and for about 30 minutes, or until toothpick inserted in the center comes out clean. Cool then fill with Orange Filling.

Orange Filling
> ½ cup sugar
> 1 egg
> Juice and zest of 1 orange
> 1 cup water
> 2 tablespoons flour
> 1 tablespoon butter

Beat sugar and egg together until light. Beat in orange juice and zest. Whisk together water and flour in the top of a double boiler and cook until mixture thickens, whisking constantly. Pour a little of the hot mixture into the sugar mixture then return all to the double boiler, whisking constantly. Cook, whisking constantly, for about 4 minutes, or until mixture thickens. Remove from heat and stir in butter.

Lillian L. Dickinson

Wedding Cake

Four pounds flour of love,
One and one half pounds of buttered youth,
One and one half pounds good looks,
One and one half pounds sweet temper,
One and one half pounds blindness of faults,
One and one half pounds sifted forgetfulness,
One and one half pounds powdered wits,
One and one half pounds dry humor,
Two tablespoonfuls sweet argument,
One and one half pints of rippling laughter,
One and one half wineglasses full common sense.

Put the flour of love, good looks and sweet temper in a well furnished house. Beat the butter of youth to cream. Mix together blindness of faults. Sift forgetfulness, powdered wits and dry humor into a sweet argument, then add this to the above. Pour in gently rippling laughter and common sense. Work it all together and bake gently forever.

Ralph M. Wade

LIZZIE ROBB'S DEVILS CAKE

½ cup unsweetened chocolate,
    chopped
½ cup boiling water
1 teaspoon baking soda
2 cups sugar
½ cup butter
2 eggs
1 cup buttermilk or sour milk
1 teaspoon vanilla
3 cups flour
1 teaspoon baking powder
Sweetened whipped cream

Preheat oven to 350 degrees. Butter and flour three 8-inch round cake pans.

Pour boiling water over chocolate to melt, stir in baking soda and set aside. In a large bowl, cream sugar and butter until fluffy. Add eggs, buttermilk and vanilla and beat until smooth. Sift together the flour and baking powder and add to creamed mixture, blending well. Stir in chocolate mixture. Pour batter into prepared pans and bake about 20 to 30 minutes, or until toothpick inserted in the center comes out clean. Cool completely. Fill with sweetened whipped cream.

Lillian L. Dickinson

BLACKBERRY JAM CAKE

1½ cups sugar
⅔ cup butter
1 cup buttermilk
3 eggs, separated
1 cup blackberry jam or jelly, seedless
1 teaspoon vanilla
3 cups flour
2 teaspoons baking powder
1 teaspoon baking soda
1 teaspoon cinnamon
⅓ teaspoon salt
½ teaspoon cloves

Butter Frosting

3 tablespoons butter, softened
1¼ cups powdered sugar
½ teaspoon vanilla
1 tablespoon milk

Preheat oven to 350 degrees. Butter and flour a 13x9-inch baking dish.

In a large bowl, cream sugar and butter together. Stir in buttermilk, egg yolks, jam and vanilla. Sift together flour, baking powder, baking soda, cinnamon, salt and cloves and stir into creamed mixture until smooth. Beat egg whites until stiff, then gently fold into batter. Pour batter into prepared pan and bake for 30 to 40 minutes, or until toothpick inserted in the center comes out clean. When cake is completely cool, spread with Butter Frosting.

For the Butter Frosting: Cream together the butter and powdered sugar until smooth. Beat in vanilla and milk.

Vernice Roberts

GRANDMA MEACHAM'S COFFEE CAKE

1 cup shortening
1 cup sugar
3 eggs
1 cup molasses
1 cup strong coffee, cooled
4½ cups flour
1 teaspoon baking soda
1 teaspoon allspice
1 teaspoon cinnamon
½ teaspoon nutmeg
1 cup nuts, chopped
1 cup currants
1 cup raisins
½ cup citron, chopped

Preheat oven to 350 degrees. Grease two 9x5x3-inch loaf pans.

In a large bowl, cream together the shortening, sugar and eggs. Stir in the molasses and coffee until blended. Sift together the flour, baking soda, allspice, cinnamon and nutmeg and add to creamed mixture and beat until smooth. Stir in nuts, currants, raisins and citron. Pour batter into prepared pans and bake for about 45 minutes, or until toothpick inserted in the center comes out clean.

Elizabeth Redington Meacham Stewart

Best Fruit Cake Ever

1 cup butter
1 cup sugar
4 large eggs
1 cup dried fruit
1 teaspoon baking powder
1 teaspoon baking soda
1 teaspoon salt
Lemon juice
1 cup brown sugar
Nuts
1 or 2 quarts whisky

Before you start, sample the whiskey to check for quality. Good, isn't it? Now go ahead.

Select a large mixing bowl, measuring cup, etc. Check the whiskey again as it must be just right. To be sure the whiskey is of the highest quality, pour 1 level cup into a glass and drink it as fast as you can. Repeat.

With an electric mixer, beat 1 cup butter in a large fluffy bowl. Add 1 teaspoon of thugar and beat again.

Meanwhile, make sure that the whiskey is of the finest quality. Cry another tup. Open second quart if nethethary.

Add 2 arge leggs, 2 cups fried druit and beat 'til high. If druit gets stuck in beaters, just pry it loose with a drewscriver. Sample the whiskey, checking for tonscisticity.

Next, sift 3 cups of salt or anything. It doesn't really matter. Sample the whiskey again.

Sift ½ pint lemon juice, fold in chopped butter and strained nuts. Add 1 babblespoon of brown thugar, or whatever color you can find, and mix well. Grease roven and turn cake pan to 350 gradees. Now pour the whole mess into roven and ake. Check the viskey again and bo to ged.

Lois Hall

59

EGG NOG CAKE

2 cups flour
1¼ cups sugar
2 teaspoons baking powder
1½ teaspoons nutmeg
1 teaspoon salt
3 eggs
1½ cups heavy cream
3 teaspoons rum or rum flavoring

Preheat oven to 350 degrees. Butter and flour a 9x9-inch pan.

In a large bowl, combine all ingredients and beat until smooth. Pour into prepared pan and bake for 30 to 40 minutes, or until toothpick inserted in the center comes out clean.

Vernice Roberts

Delicious Cake Recipe

This recipe is from my great-grandmother, Susannah Hankins, who came across the Oregon Trail in a covered wagon in 1852. This recipe, in Susannah's own words, has been passed down and enjoyed by seven generations of my family.

Without milk, eggs or butter. Put into the saucepan the following and boil three minutes, then cool: one cup each of brown sugar; water and seeded raisins; scant one-third cup of lard, one-fourth small nutmeg; one half teaspoon each of cinnamon and cloves. After cooled (not cold) stir in one teaspoon of soda dissolved in a little warm water. Then stir in two cups of flour with one half teaspoon baking powder and nuts if desired and bake in a loaf form or in dripping pan. Bake in 350 oven about 45 minutes or so. Test by using a broom straw in center of cake to see if done.

Ethel Conn Schneider

GINGERBREAD

½ cup sugar
¼ cup light molasses
¼ cup shortening
1 egg
1 teaspoon baking soda
½ teaspoon cinnamon
½ teaspoon ginger
¼ teaspoon salt
½ cup boiling water
1 cup flour
¼ cup brown sugar
¼ cup nuts, chopped

Preheat oven to 350 degrees. Butter and flour an 8x8-inch cake pan.

In a large bowl, cream together the sugar, molasses, shortening and egg. Dissolve the baking soda, cinnamon, ginger and salt in the boiling water. Add to creamed mixture alternately with the flour, beating well after each addition. Pour batter into prepared pan. Combine brown sugar and nuts and sprinkle over the top. Bake for about 25 minutes, or until toothpick inserted in the center comes out clean.

Ethel Wiggins Reynolds
Jane Reynolds Hyatt
Mary Westmorland

CHEESE CAKE

2 cups cream cheese
1 cup heavy cream
1½ tablespoons flour
6 eggs, separated
1 cup sugar
1 teaspoon vanilla
Zest of half a lemon
Pastry for a single crust pie

Preheat oven to 350 degrees. Line a 10-inch springform pan with pastry.

In a large bowl, blend cream cheese and cream until smooth. Sift the flour into cream mixture and stir. In a separate bowl, beat the egg yolks and sugar until very light and thick. Add to cream mixture and stir until smooth. Stir in vanilla and lemon zest. Beat the egg whites until stiff then gently fold into mixture. Pour filling into prepared pastry and bake about 45 minutes, or until filling is set. Chill before serving.

Gerald W. Frank

AUBLE COOGAN

My great-grandmother, Margaret Bergmann, made this moist German apple cake and handed it down through the family. Margaret and her husband Theodore Edward Bergmann came to Oregon from Germany and founded the Bergmann shoe factory in Portland. He became known for the Bergmann logging boot, and the loggers wouldn't be without them.

1½ cups flour
2 teaspoons baking powder
¼ teaspoon salt
1 cup sugar
½ cup milk
2 eggs, beaten
3 tablespoons melted butter
1 teaspoon vanilla
2 apples; peeled, cored and sliced
1 tablespoon sugar
1 teaspoon cinnamon
2 eggs
2 tablespoons sugar
2 tablespoons milk

Preheat oven to 350 degrees. Butter a 10-inch pie plate.

In a large bowl, sift together the flour, baking powder and salt. Add 1 cup sugar, ½ cup milk, 2 eggs, butter and vanilla and beat until well blended. Pour batter into prepared pan and arrange apple slices over batter. Combine 1 tablespoon sugar and cinnamon and sprinkle over apples. Bake for 25 minutes. Combine the remaining 2 eggs, 2 tablespoons sugar and 2 tablespoons milk. Spread on the cake and bake an additional 10 minutes, or until topping is set.

Sally (Springer) Madden

Scripture Cake

This is from my great-grandmother, Alpha L. Robinson, who came to the Oregon Country from Missouri in a covered wagon with her parents, the William Robinsons', in 1878. The Indians they met were always friendly.

You will need a Bible to decipher the ingredients, enjoy the puzzle!

Two cupfuls of Jeremiah, 6 Chapter,
     20 Verse
One and one half cupfuls of
     Judges 5:25, last clause
One half cupful of 1 Kings 4:22
Two cupfuls of Samuel 30:12
Two cupfuls of Nahum 3:12
One cupful of Numbers 17:8
One half cupful of Judges 4:19,
     last clause
Two tablespoons of Samuel 14:25
Two teaspoonfuls of Amos 4:5
Season to taste with 2 Chronicles 9:9
Add six of Jeremiah 17:11

Follow Solomon's prescription for making a good boy, Proverbs 23:14, and you will have a good loaf cake.

Marlene Makinson Pollard

POVERTY CAKE

My grandmother, Rose Schweigert Rose, homesteaded in the Hood River valley in 1913. She had received her nursing degree and, during the early years, was the only person with medical training in the area. She was called upon to deliver many babies and give nursing care in countless situations.

1 cup sugar
½ cup butter
1 cup buttermilk or sour milk
1 teaspoon salvation (baking soda)
1½ cups flour
1 teaspoon cinnamon
¼ teaspoon nutmeg
1 cup raisins

Preheat oven to 350 degrees. Grease a 9x5x3-inch loaf pan.

In a large bowl, cream together the sugar and butter until light. In a separate bowl, dissolve baking soda in the buttermilk, then blend with the sugar mixture. Sift together the flour, cinnamon and nutmeg then stir into batter until smooth. Stir in raisins. Pour batter into prepared pan and bake for about 45 minutes, or until toothpick inserted in the center comes out clean.

Carolyn Rust Langtry

Apple Snow

Peel and core 10 apples. Simmer in 1 cup water with 1 lemon rind until tender. Put through colander and cool. Take 10 egg whites, beat to a stiff froth, and fold into apples. Add ½ pound of pulverized sugar, and continue beating till stiff. Serve in a glass dish with either custard sauce made with egg yolks or whipped cream. This is good enough for a party when served with sponge cake.

Lynda Hatch

OLD RAISIN CAKE

This wonderful recipe came with my family in a covered wagon from Minnesota to Oregon on the northern route through Montana. My grandmother used ingredients available on the Trail. The recipe does not take milk, a rare commodity on the Trail, and fresh eggs were scarce although wild fowl eggs were sometimes found.

1 pound raisins or other dried fruit
    such as prunes or apples
2 cups hot water
1½ cups sugar
½ cup shortening or lard
2 eggs (optional)
3 cups flour
1 teaspoon baking powder
1 teaspoon baking soda
1 teaspoon cinnamon
1 teaspoon nutmeg
½ teaspoon cloves
½ teaspoon salt
1 cup nuts, chopped

Preheat oven to 350 degrees. Grease a 13x9-inch pan.

Combine raisins, water, sugar and shortening in a saucepan and bring to a boil. Boil for 10 minutes, stirring often. Cool completely. Beat in eggs, flour, baking powder, baking soda, cinnamon, nutmeg, cloves and salt until smooth. Stir in nuts. Pour batter into prepared pan and bake about 45 minutes, or until toothpick inserted in the center comes out clean.

Shirley Brady Camp

WALNUT CAKE

10 eggs, separated
1 cup sugar
1½ cups walnuts, finely ground
Juice and zest of ½ lemon

Preheat oven to 325.

In a large bowl, beat the egg yolks and sugar together for 30 minutes. Stir in the ground walnuts, lemon juice and zest. Beat egg whites until stiff and gently fold into batter, taking care not to deflate egg whites. Pour into an ungreased 10-inch springform pan. Bake for about 40 minutes. Spread with Miss Tracy's Frosting.

Gerald W. Frank

MISS TRACY'S FROSTING

1 egg white
1 cup powdered sugar
1 tablespoon lemon juice
½ teaspoon vanilla

Beat the egg white until frothy then beat in the powdered sugar gradually. Add lemon juice and vanilla then beat until thick.

Gerald W. Frank

BROD TORTE

10 eggs, separated
½ cup sugar
Juice and zest of 1 lemon
6 ounces almonds, finely ground
3 tablespoons matzos meal
1¼ teaspoons cinnamon
½ teaspoon cloves
⅛ teaspoon salt
1 apple; peeled, cored and grated

Preheat oven to 350 degrees. Butter a 10-inch springform pan.

In a large bowl, beat together the egg yolks and sugar until very thick and light. Stir in lemon juice and zest, matzos meal, cinnamon, cloves, salt and apple until smooth. Beat egg whites until stiff and fold into batter. Pour into prepared pan and bake about 40 minutes, or until toothpick inserted in the center comes out clean.

Gerald W. Frank

DATE NUT TORTE

12 eggs, beaten
4 cups sugar
2 cups cake flour
1 teaspoon salt
1 teaspoon vanilla
4 cups dates, chopped
4 cups nuts, chopped

Preheat oven to 350 degrees. Butter and flour a 13x9x3-inch baking dish.

In a large bowl, beat eggs until frothy. Beat in sugar until mixture thickens. Sift flour and salt together then fold into mixture. Fold in vanilla, dates and nuts. Pour into prepared baking dish and bake for about 35 minutes, or until toothpick inserted in the center comes out clean.

Don Daniels
Diane Daniels

OLD ENGLISH RUM CAKE

Don Daniels was Meier & Franks' Chef in the Georgian Room, Tea Room and the Men's Grill for 48 years.

2 cups butter
2 cups sugar
12 eggs
4 cups flour
1 teaspoon baking powder
1 teaspoon salt
2 cups almonds, chopped
2 cups filberts, chopped
1¼ cups maraschino cherries
¼ cup Jamaican Rum

Preheat oven to 350 degrees. Butter and flour three 9x5x3-inch loaf pans.

In a large bowl, cream together the butter and sugar until light. Add eggs, one at a time, beating well after each addition. Stir in flour, baking powder and salt until smooth. Stir in almonds, filberts, cherries and rum until combined. Pour into prepared pans and bake for about 30 minutes, or until toothpick inserted in the center comes out clean.

Don Daniels
Diane Daniels

COCONUT CAKE

6 egg yolks, well beaten
2 cups powdered sugar
¾ cup butter, softened
1 cup milk
3½ cups flour
2 teaspoons cream of tartar
1 teaspoon baking soda
4 egg whites, beaten until stiff

Coconut Icing:
2 egg whites
1 cup powdered sugar
¾ cup shredded coconut

Preheat oven to 350 degrees. Butter and flour two 8-inch cake pans.

In a large bowl, beat together the egg yolks and powdered sugar until light. Add butter and milk and stir. Sift together flour, cream of tartar and baking soda and beat into mixture until smooth. Gently fold in stiffly beaten egg whites. Pour into prepared pans, and bake for about 25 minutes, or until toothpick inserted in center comes out clean. Cool cakes completely and frost with Coconut Icing.

For the Coconut Icing: Beat 2 egg whites until stiff, then stir in the powdered sugar, ¼ cup at a time, until incorporated. Fold in the coconut. Frost cake, then bake at 350 degrees for about 10 minutes, or until icing is barely golden.

Eva Emery Dye
Dolly Hutchinson

BURNT LEATHER CAKE

My grandfather was one-year old when he came across the Oregon Trail with the Morely family in 1847. They took a Donation Land Claim in the Waldo Hills, just east of Salem, Oregon. My grandmother, Liza Jane Givens Morely, came with her family from Ontario, Canada, by riverboat and covered wagon in the 1850s. They were strong and brave people.

Caramel Syrup:
>   1 cup brown sugar
>   ½ cup boiling water

Cake:
>   1½ cups sugar
>   ½ cup butter
>   4 egg yolks
>   1 cup water
>   2½ cups flour
>   4 tablespoons Caramel Syrup
>   1 teaspoon vanilla
>   ½ cup flour
>   2 teaspoons baking powder
>   2 egg whites, stiffly beaten

Burnt Leather Icing:
>   1½ cups sugar
>   ½ cup water
>   2 egg whites, stiffly beaten
>   1 teaspoon vanilla

Preheat oven to 375 degrees. Grease two 9-inch round cake pans.

For the Caramel Syrup: Melt brown sugar in a heavy saucepan, stirring constantly. When sugar just starts to burn, very slowly pour in boiling water and stir well. Boil syrup until it is the consistency of molasses. Cool.

For the Cake: In a large bowl, cream together the sugar and butter until fluffy. Beat in egg yolks, one at a time, beating well after each addition. Add 1 cup water and 2½ cups flour and beat for 5 minutes. Stir in the 4 tablespoons of Caramel Syrup and vanilla. Sift ½ cup flour and baking powder into cake mixture and blend well. Fold in stiffly beaten egg whites. Pour into prepared cake pans and bake for about 25 minutes, or until toothpick inserted in the center comes out clean. Cool com-pletely, then fill and frost with the Burnt Leather Icing.

For the Burnt Leather Icing:
Combine 1½ cups sugar and ½ cup water in a heavy sauce pan. Boil until the soft crack stage, 270 degrees. Remove from heat and stir in remaining Caramel Syrup. Pour hot syrup in a thin stream into beaten egg whites and whisk until very smooth. Whisk in vanilla. Allow to cool then fill and frost cake.

Jane Downs

PRUNE CAKE

This cake was made by my grandmother, Nellie Smyth, in the 1800s.

>   ¾ cup butter
>   1½ cups sugar
>   2½ cups flour
>   1 teaspoon baking soda
>   1 teaspoon cinnamon
>   1 teaspoon cloves
>   ¼ cup sour milk or buttermilk
>   3 eggs
>   ⅓ cup water
>   1 cup cooked prunes, pitted and
>   chopped

Preheat oven to 375 degrees. Grease a 9x13-inch pan.

In a large bowl, cream butter and sugar together until light and fluffy. Sift flour, baking soda, cinnamon and cloves into the butter mixture. Add buttermilk, eggs and water then beat until smooth. Stir in prunes. Pour in to prepared pan and bake for about 35 minutes, or until toothpick inserted in the center comes out clean.

Marie Moore Hardin

Dried Apples Fruit Cake

This recipe was brought along the Applegate Trail in a covered wagon in 1846, by my great-great-grandmother, Mary Elizabeth Boone Norris.

Soak 3 cups dried apples overnight in cold water. In the morning chop them. Add 3 cups molasses. Stew until almost soft. Add 1 cup raisins. Let cool and add to cake. Cream together 1 cup butter and lard mixed and brown sugar, 3 eggs, 1 teaspoon soda. Spices to taste. Flour enough to make a stiff batter.

Aileen Barker Rickard

FAMOUS BROWNIES

5 1-ounce squares unsweetened chocolate
½ cup butter
6 eggs
4 cups sugar
½ teaspoon salt
½ teaspoon vanilla
½ cup flour
2 cups nuts, chopped

Preheat oven to 325 degrees. Butter a 13x9-inch baking dish.

Melt chocolate and butter together in the top of a double-boiler over barely simmering water. Cool. In a large bowl, beat eggs until frothy. Add sugar and beat until very thick and pale colored. Stir in salt and vanilla. Stir in flour and mix well. Stir in nuts. Pour into prepared baking dish and bake for about 45 minutes, or just until toothpick inserted in the center comes out clean.

Don Daniels
Diane Daniels

ROSE GERANIUM CAKE

My family moved West from Tennessee and the Great Smoky Mountain area because of the opportunities in mining and farming; and because they felt that the Civil War was inevitable. They brought this recipe for a simple cake with a unique flavoring. Seasonings like vanilla were hard to come by so they used available plants to flavor foods. I can remember "helping" by placing the rose geranium leaves in the greased cake pan just before the batter was poured over them.

1½ cups flour
⅔ cup sugar
2 teaspoons baking powder
½ teaspoon salt
⅓ cup butter, softened
⅔ cup milk
1 egg
Rose geranium leaves

Icing:
2 tablespoons milk
1 teaspoon fresh rose geranium leaves, minced
⅔ cup powdered sugar

Preheat oven to 350 degrees. Grease an 8-inch cake pan.

Sift flour, sugar, baking powder and salt into a large bowl and make a well in the center. Add the butter and half of the milk; beat until smooth. Add the remaining milk and the egg; beat for 1 minute or until smooth. Place several rose geranium leaves in the bottom of prepared pan and pour in batter. Bake for 30 minutes or until toothpick inserted in the center comes out clean. Turn out onto a rack to cool. Spread with icing while still warm.

For the Icing: Combine milk with the minced rose geranium leaves and let steep 30 minutes. Strain flavor infused milk into powdered sugar and beat until smooth. Use to ice cake.

Carol Speer Jordison

BOILED SPICE CAKE

This is one of my favorite recipes from my grandmother, Nellie Helmick Curry.

2 cups sugar
2 cups water
2 cups raisins
1 cup lard or shortening
2 teaspoons cinnamon
2 teaspoons cloves
1 teaspoon salt
2 cups flour
2 teaspoons baking soda
1 cup nuts, chopped

Preheat oven to 350 degrees. Grease a 9x5-inch loaf pan.

Combine sugar, water, raisins, lard, cinnamon, cloves and salt in a sauce pan. Bring to a boil, stirring constantly. Remove from heat and let cool slightly. Stir in flour, baking soda and nuts until smooth. Pour into prepared pan and bake for 50 minutes, or until toothpick inserted in the center comes out clean.

Lynne Hanson

POTATO CAKE

My mother, Myrtle Smyth Barnes, made this cake for as long as I can remember.

3 cups sugar
2/3 cup butter
4 eggs
1 cup walnuts, chopped
2 cups flour
1/2 cup milk
1 teaspoon baking powder
1 cup hot mashed potatoes
1/2 cup cocoa
1 teaspoon cinnamon

Preheat oven to 375 degrees. Butter and flour a 9x13-inch pan.

Combine all ingredients beat until smooth. Pour into prepared pan and bake for about 40 minutes, or until toothpick inserted in the center comes out clean.

Marie Moore Hardin

AUNT INDE'S CREAM CAKE

My great-grandfather, Henry Jones, traveled the Oregon Trail in 1853.

1¼ cups whipping cream
1 cup sugar
2 eggs, well beaten
1 teaspoon vanilla
2 cups cake flour
2 teaspoons baking powder
½ teaspoon salt
1 cup whipping cream
2 tablespoons sugar

Preheat oven to 350 degrees. Butter and flour two 9-inch cake pans.

Pour 1¼ cups whipping cream into a large bowl. Whip the cream until light and fluffy then fold in sugar. Stir in eggs and vanilla. Sift together the flour, baking powder and salt then fold into the cream mixture. Stir gently until smooth. Pour into prepared pans and bake for 25 to 30 minutes, or until toothpick inserted in the center comes out clean. Cool completely.

Pour remaining 1 cup whipping cream into a bowl and whip the cream until soft peaks form. Whisk in the remaining 2 tablespoons sugar. Frost the cake with the sweetened whipped cream.

Bonnie C. Brown

GRANDMA HATFIELD'S APPLESAUCE FRUITCAKE

2½ cups unsweetened applesauce,
    warmed
1 cup shortening
4 teaspoons baking soda
2 cups sugar
1 teaspoon baking powder
1 teaspoon salt
1 teaspoon cinnamon
1 teaspoon cloves
½ teaspoon nutmeg
4½ cups flour
1½ cups nuts, chopped
1½ cups chopped, candied fruit,
    (apples, pears, cherries)
1 cup raisins

Preheat oven to 325 degrees. Grease two 9x5-inch loaf pans.

Combine the hot applesauce and shortening in a large bowl, and stir until the shortening is melted. Stir in the baking soda and let cool. Add remaining ingredients and stir until well blended. Pour into prepared pans and bake for about 1 hour and 15 minutes, or until toothpick inserted in the center comes out clean. When completely cool, wrap well in foil and store in refrigerator. Will keep for about two months.

Jacqueline Wilson

DUTCH BUTTER CAKE

1 cup butter, salted
1 cup sugar
2 cups flour
1 egg
1 teaspoon almond extract
¼ cup slivered almonds

Preheat oven to 325 degrees for glass pie plate, or 350 degrees for tin pie plate.

Soften butter for 2 hours at room temperature. In a large bowl, mix butter and sugar with a wooden spoon. Mix in flour. Add egg and almond extract and mix well. Gather into a large, soft ball and knead lightly. Press into a pie plate, then press slivered almonds into dough. Bake for 35 minutes or until delicately brown. Serve in small wedges.

Ria Nauta

CRUMB CAKE

My grandparents, Mr. and Mrs. Patrick Murphy, came to Oregon around 1900. He died of an accident but she lived to be almost 102 years old. This is her recipe. I have made it many, many times and still do.

2 cups brown sugar
2½ cups flour
¾ cup lard or shortening
1 cup sour milk or buttermilk
1 egg
1 teaspoon baking soda
½ teaspoon cinnamon
½ teaspoon cloves
1 cup raisins

Preheat oven to 350 degrees. Grease an 8x8-inch pan.

Combine brown sugar, flour and lard in a large bowl. Rub together until mixture resembles coarse meal. Set aside 1 cup of this mixture for the topping. To the remaining mixture, add rest of ingredients and mix well. Spread batter in prepared pan and sprinkle over reserved topping. Bake for about 35 minutes.

Myra Ferris

APPLESAUCE CAKE

2 cups applesauce
½ cup melted lard, (or shortening)
1 cup sugar
2 cups flour
1½ tablespoons cocoa powder
1½ teaspoons baking soda
1 teaspoon cinnamon
1 teaspoon nutmeg
1 teaspoon cloves
½ cup raisins
½ cup nuts, chopped

Preheat oven to 350 degrees. Butter and lightly flour two 8-inch round pans or one 9x13-inch baking dish.

In a large bowl, beat the applesauce, lard and sugar together. In a separate bowl sift the flour, cocoa, baking soda, cinnamon, nutmeg and cloves. Stir into applesauce mixture until well blended. Stir in raisins and nuts. Spread batter into prepared pans and bake, about 25-30 minutes for the round pans, 35-40 minutes for the rectangle. Test to see if done by inserting a toothpick in the center, it should come out clean.

Irene Mead

EGGLESS, MILKLESS, BUTTERLESS CAKE

Nora Colton lived in the Medical Springs area of Baker County, Oregon. She raised fifteen children, eight girls and seven boys. They ran sheep, at one time had three bands. This is one of her favorite receipts.

2 cups water
2 cups brown sugar
2 cups raisins
1 cup shortening
2 teaspoons cloves
2 teaspoons nutmeg
1 teaspoon salt
4 cups flour
2 teaspoons baking powder
2 teaspoons baking soda

Preheat oven to 350 degrees. Grease two 8-inch round cake pans.

In a large saucepan, combine water, brown sugar, raisins, shortening, cloves, nutmeg and salt. Bring to a boil then reduce heat to medium and simmer, stirring often, for three minutes. Remove from heat and cool completely. Sift together flour, baking powder and baking soda and gradually stir into the other ingredients. Stir the batter until smooth. Pour into prepared pans. Bake for approximately one hour or until a toothpick inserted in the middle comes out clean.

Eloise Colton

GRANDMA OLD'S NUT CAKE

1 cup sugar
½ cup butter
1⅓ cups flour
1½ teaspoons baking powder
½ cup coffee, cooled
3 egg whites
1 cup walnuts, coarsely chopped

Preheat oven to 350 degrees. Butter and lightly flour a 9x5x3-inch loaf pan.

Cream sugar and butter until light. Sift together flour and baking powder. Add flour mixture alternately with the coffee to the sugar mixture, stirring well after each addition. Beat egg whites until stiff then fold into batter. Stir in walnuts. Pour batter into prepared pan and bake for approximately 40 minutes or until toothpick inserted in the center comes out clean.

Marjorie Nahouse Stewart

WIND CAKE

4 eggs, separated
¾ cup cold water
1¼ cups sugar
1 teaspoon vanilla
½ cup flour
¾ teaspoon cream of tartar

Preheat oven to 350 degrees.
Beat the egg yolks with the cold water until foamy. Gradually add the sugar, stirring until blended. Stir in vanilla. Sift flour and fold in gently. In a separate bowl, beat the egg whites until they hold soft peaks. Add cream of tartar and continue beating until stiff. Carefully fold into other mixture. Pour batter into an ungreased 9-inch tube pan and bake for approximately 45 minutes.

Chris Rossi

BROWNIES

2 eggs, beaten
1¼ cups brown sugar
½ teaspoon vanilla
½ cup flour
¼ teaspoon salt
¼ cup butter, melted
2 ounces unsweetened chocolate
½ cup walnuts, chopped

Preheat oven to 300 degrees. Lightly grease an 8x8-inch baking pan.
Combine all ingredients in a large bowl and beat until smooth. Spread batter evenly in prepared pan and bake about 30 minutes, or until toothpick inserted in the center comes out clean.

Karen Eoff Baker

MOTHER'S GINGERBREAD

My mother, who was born in 1885, passed this old, handwritten family recipe on to me. As a child, I remember how often we had warm gingerbread with mounds of whipping cream during the weeks between Thanksgiving and New Years. Why then? Because an elderly German neighbor always spent the long holiday season with relatives out of town. During his absence, my daddy milked his cows for him and our family got all of the milk to use. Mother set shallow pans of milk in our pantry, then skimmed off the cream for whipping.

½ cup sugar
¼ cup butter
¼ cup lard or shortening
2½ cups flour
1½ teaspoons baking soda
1 teaspoon cinnamon
1 teaspoon ground ginger
½ teaspoon ground cloves
½ teaspoon salt
1 cup molasses
1 egg, beaten
1 cup boiling water

Preheat oven to 350 degrees. Grease a 9x9-inch pan.

In a large bowl, cream sugar, butter and lard together until light. Sift together flour, baking soda, cinnamon, ginger, cloves and salt together into sugar mixture. Add molasses and egg and beat until smooth. Add boiling water and beat until smooth. Pour into prepared pan and bake for 50 to 60 minutes, or until toothpick inserted in center comes out clean.

Esther Fredenburg

APPLESAUCE CAKE WITH PENUCHE ICING

¾ cup raisins
½ cup boiling water
1½ cups dark brown sugar, packed
½ cup shortening
2 eggs
1 teaspoon salt
½ teaspoon cinnamon
½ teaspoon cloves
½ teaspoon allspice
1½ cups thick applesauce
2½ cups flour, sifted
¾ cups walnuts, chopped
2 teaspoons baking soda

Preheat oven to 350 degrees. Grease and flour a 13x9x2-inch pan.

Combine raisins and boiling water, set aside. In a large bowl, beat brown sugar, shortening, eggs, salt, cinnamon, cloves and allspice together until smooth and fluffy. Scrape bowl often. Stir in applesauce, then flour and walnuts. Stir baking soda into undrained raisins. Add to batter and mix well. Pour into prepared pan and bake for 40 to 45 minutes, or until toothpick inserted in the center comes out clean. Cool completely. Frost with Penuche Icing (below).

Penuche Icing

½ cup butter
1 cup brown sugar, packed
¼ cup milk
1¾ to 2 cups powdered sugar, sifted

Melt butter in a saucepan over low heat. Stir in brown sugar and bring to a boil, stirring constantly. Boil for 2 minutes, stirring constantly. Stir in milk and return to a boil, stirring constantly. Remove from heat and cool to lukewarm. Gradually stir in powdered sugar and beat until cool and thick.

Roberta Seeber

Cookies & Candies

GRANDMA SENGER'S SUGAR COOKIES

2 cups sugar
1 cup butter, softened
2 eggs
1 cup sour cream
2 teaspoons vanilla
1 teaspoon baking soda
8 cups flour
Sugar for sprinkling

Preheat oven to 375 degrees. Grease several baking sheets.

Cream together the sugar and butter until light. Beat in eggs. Add sour cream, vanilla and baking soda and stir until well combined. Stir in flour. Chill dough 3 to 4 hours before rolling. Turn out dough on lightly floured board and roll out to about 1/8-inch thickness. Cut into desired shapes and score lightly with the tines of a fork in a criss-cross pattern. Sprinkle with sugar. Place on greased baking sheets and bake for 7 to 12 minutes.

Sandra L. Stanley

SHORTBREAD FROM FORT VANCOUVER

2 cups flour
2 tablespoons sugar
1/4 teaspoon salt
1/2 cup butter
Sugar for sprinkling

Preheat oven to 325 degrees.

Sift the flour, sugar and salt together into a large bowl. Cut the butter into pieces and rub into the flour mixture until it resembles coarse meal. Knead very lightly to form dough. Roll out on a lightly floured board into a 7 or 8-inch circle. Carefully lift with a spatula and place on an ungreased baking sheet. Decoratively scallop edges and mark the top into six portions. Prick the top with a fork and sprinkle with sugar. Bake for about 40 minutes or until it is pale golden. Cool on rack.

Rick Edwards
Park Ranger
Fort Vancouver National Historic Site

PENUCHE FROM GRANDMA NAHOUSE

4 cups sugar
1 cup milk
2 tablespoons butter
1 cup walnuts, chopped

Lightly oil an 8x8-inch pan.

Combine sugar, milk and butter in a heavy saucepan, stirring to mix well. Cook slowly to the soft-ball stage, 234 degrees. Remove from heat and beat until smooth and creamy. Stir in the walnuts then pour into the prepared pan to cool. When firm, cut into pieces. Store in airtight container.

Marjorie Nahouse Stewart

JUMBO OAT COOKIES

3/4 cup sugar
1/3 cup margarine or butter
1/3 cup corn syrup
2 egg whites, slightly beaten
1 teaspoon almond extract
2 1/4 cups oatmeal
1 cup flour
3 tablespoons sliced almonds
1/2 teaspoon baking soda
1/2 teaspoon salt

Preheat oven to 350 degrees.

Beat sugar, margarine and corn syrup together until fluffy. Add egg whites and almond extract and mix well. Stir in remaining ingredients and mix well. Drop by 1/4 cupful of cookie dough 2-inches apart onto ungreased cookie sheet. Bake for 14 to 16 minutes.

Janice M. Hardy

Sugar was a scarce commodity in the Oregon Territory in the 1850s. Molasses, honey or brown sugar were commonly used, and what little refined or white sugar that the family had was saved for "special" company.

One day little Clara had the hiccups. All of the old wive's tales were tried but none of them stopped the child's spasms. Finally Elenore, who was a rather stern person and not given to joking, turned to Clara and in her sternest voice said, "Clara, have you been eating the sugar?" This scared Clara so much that her hiccups were immediately stopped.

Clara M. Foster

HONEY CLUSTERS

2 cups flour
¼ teaspoon salt
3 eggs
1 teaspoon vanilla
Oil for frying
½ cup honey
½ cup sugar

Sift flour and salt into a large mixing bowl and make a well in the center. Add eggs, one at a time, beating well after each addition. Add vanilla and mix until you have a soft dough. Turn out onto a lightly floured board and knead until satiny and resilient. Divide dough in half and roll out to ¼-inch thick. Cut strips ¼-inch wide. Using the palms of your hands, roll the strips to the thickness of a pencil. Cut into ½-inch lengths.

Heat oil in a skillet to 360 degrees. Fry in hot oil, one layer deep, do not crowd. When golden brown, turn to cook the other side. When golden on all sides, remove from hot oil and drain on absorbent paper towels.

Heat honey and sugar in a heavy skillet over medium heat for 5 minutes. Remove from heat and stir in deep-fried cookies. Stir to coat all sides with honey-sugar mixture then remove with slotted spoon and allow to cool.

Silvia Brown

HERMITS

½ cup butter, softened
¾ cup brown sugar, packed
1 egg
½ cup light molasses
1½ cups flour
½ teaspoon cinnamon
½ teaspoon nutmeg
½ teaspoon cloves
½ teaspoon baking soda
¼ teaspoon salt
1½ cups raisins
¾ cup walnuts, chopped

Preheat oven to 350 degrees. Grease two baking sheets.

In a large mixing bowl cream butter and sugar together until light and fluffy. Beat in egg then molasses. Sift together flour, cinnamon, nutmeg, cloves, baking soda and salt. Add to the butter mixture and beat thoroughly. Stir in raisins and walnuts. Drop by teaspoonfuls onto baking sheet. Bake until top is firm and center is chewy, about 8 to 10 minutes.

Mrs. Jacquie Young

MOLASSES COOKIES

My family came to Oregon very early in its history. Many of my recipes have been handed down from my grandmother who was born in Silverton, Oregon in 1863. Her parents came here with the army. There were thirteen children in the Dent family so we have kinfolk all over Oregon and Washington.

1/2 cup shortening
1/2 cup sugar
1 egg
1 cup dark molasses
1 tablespoon lemon juice
3 1/2 cups flour
2 teaspoons baking powder
1 teaspoon cinnamon
3/4 teaspoon ground cloves
1/2 teaspoon ground ginger
1/2 teaspoon salt
1/3 cup boiling water
Sugar for sprinkling

Preheat oven to 350 degrees. Grease baking sheets.

In a large bowl cream together shortening and sugar. Add egg and beat well. Blend in molasses and lemon juice. Sift together flour, baking powder, cinnamon, cloves, ginger and salt then add to creamed mixture and blend well. Add boiling water and stir to mix well. Chill dough. Drop by teaspoonfuls onto greased baking sheets and sprinkle with sugar. Bake 8 to 10 minutes.

Marie High

PATIENCE CANDY

3 cups sugar, in all
2 cups cream, in all
1 tablespoon butter
1 cup chopped nuts

In a heavy skillet caramelize 1 cup of the sugar. Slowly stir in 1 cup of the cream. Bring to a boil stirring constantly. Stir in remaining sugar, cream and butter. Bring back to boil and cook without stirring until it reaches the firm ball stage, 244 degrees. Remove from heat and stir in the nuts. When cool enough to handle, lightly butter hands and form into small balls.

Araminta Phillips
Daralene Wade

77

GRANDMA GOODWIN'S COOKIES

My grandmother, Fannie Burge, came over the Oregon Trail in a covered wagon in 1864. She was six years old and it was her job to watch out for Indians from the rear of the wagon.

1 cup sugar
⅓ cup shortening
3½ cups flour
2 teaspoons baking powder
1 teaspoon salt
¼ teaspoon baking soda
¼ teaspoon nutmeg
1 cup sour cream
2 eggs
1 teaspoon vanilla
Sugar for sprinkling on top

Preheat oven to 375 degrees. Grease baking sheets.

In a large bowl, cream together sugar and shortening. In a separate bowl, sift together flour baking powder, salt, baking soda and nutmeg. In a separate bowl, blend the sour cream, eggs and vanilla. Add flour mixture and sour cream mixture alternately to the creamed mixture, beating well after each addition. Chill dough for 1 hour. Turn out dough onto a lightly floured board and roll thin. Cut out with cookie cutter and place on prepared baking sheets. Sprinkle with sugar. Bake for 8 to 12 minutes or until pale golden.

Claire Stone Belsher

PEANUT BUTTER CRISSCROSSES

1 cup margarine or butter, softened
1½ cups brown sugar, firmly packed
¾ cup sugar
2 eggs, lightly beaten
1 teaspoon vanilla
1½ cups peanut butter
2¾ cups flour
2 teaspoons baking soda

Preheat oven to 350 degrees.

In a large bowl, cream together margarine, brown sugar, sugar, eggs and vanilla until smooth. Stir in peanut butter. Sift flour and baking soda together and stir into creamed mixture. Drop by rounded teaspoonfuls onto ungreased baking sheets. Press each one flat with the back of a floured fork twice, to make a criss cross design. Bake for about 10 minutes.

Josephine Koontz

BEST CHOCOLATE PINWHEELS

½ cup butter, softened
¾ cup sugar
1 egg
1 teaspoon vanilla
1¼ cups flour
¼ teaspoon baking powder
¼ teaspoon salt
1 square unsweetened chocolate

Preheat oven to 350 degrees.

In a large bowl, cream together butter, sugar, egg and vanilla until light and fluffy. Sift together flour, baking powder and salt and stir into creamed mixture until well blended. Halve the dough. Melt unsweetened chocolate and stir into half of the dough. Chill dough for several hours to make rolling easier. Roll out white dough on a sheet of floured, waxed paper to form a 9x12-inch rectangle. Roll out chocolate dough to the same size on another piece of floured, waxed paper. Invert chocolate dough on top of white dough and peel off waxed paper. Press together gently with a rolling pin. Roll up tightly from the long side. Wrap in waxed paper and chill overnight. Slice rolls ⅛ to ¼-inch thick and place on baking sheets. Bake for about 10 minutes.

Josephine Koontz

OATMEAL COOKIES

This recipe was handed down by my grandmother, Mary Jane Wiser Mays, who was a Barlow Trail Pioneer.

1½ cups raisins
1 cup water
2 cups sugar
1½ cups shortening
4 eggs, beaten
1 teaspoon baking soda
4 cups flour
2 teaspoons cinnamon
2 teaspoons baking powder
1 teaspoon salt
4 cups oatmeal
1 to 2 cups chopped nuts, (optional)

Preheat oven to 350 degrees.

Combine raisins and water in a saucepan and bring to a boil. Remove from heat and let raisins cool in the water to plump them. Cream together sugar and shortening. Add eggs and beat until smooth. Strain raisins and reserve the liquid. Dissolve baking soda in the raisin liquid and stir into the creamed mixture. Sift together the flour, cinnamon, baking powder and salt and beat into the creamed mixture. Stir in the oatmeal. Stir in the raisins and nuts. Drop by the teaspoonfuls onto ungreased baking sheets. Bake until golden, about 12 minutes.

Estelle Mays Harbison

MOTHER'S DROP COOKIES

1 cup sugar
¾ cup butter
¾ cup buttermilk or sour milk
1 egg
1½ cups flour
3 tablespoons cocoa powder
½ teaspoon baking soda
¼ teaspoon cream of tartar
⅔ cup nuts, chopped

Preheat oven to 350 degrees. Grease baking sheets.

In a large bowl, beat sugar, butter, buttermilk and egg together until smooth. Mix the flour, cocoa, baking soda and cream of tartar together and add to the first mixture, beating well. Stir in nuts. Drop by teaspoonfuls onto prepared baking sheets and bake 10 to 12 minutes.

Carolyn Rust Langtry

DATE ROLL

Araminta Eliza Hough married Harrison Phillips and came to Oregon in 1888.

3 cups sugar
1 cup evaporated milk
8 ounces pitted dates, chopped
1 tablespoon butter
1 cup walnuts, coarsely chopped

Boil sugar and milk together to the firm ball stage, 244 degrees. Stir in remaining ingredients and remove from heat. When cool enough to handle, lightly butter hands and form into a roll. Wrap in foil and chill. Slice when firm.

Araminta Phillips
Daralene Wade

SWEDISH SPRITZ

1 pound butter, softened
1 cup sugar
1 egg
1 teaspoon vanilla
4 cups flour, sifted

Preheat oven to 400 degrees.

In a large bowl, cream together the butter and sugar until smooth. Add the egg and vanilla and beat until very light. Mix in the flour until dough is smooth.

Fit a spritz cookie press with the plate of your choice. Fill cookie press with dough and press cookies out onto ungreased cookie sheet. Bake for 10 to 12 minutes or until cookies are just barely golden.

Lisa Roberts

GINGERSNAPS

¾ cup shortening
1 cup brown sugar
¼ cup molasses
1 egg
2¼ cups flour
2 teaspoons baking soda
1 teaspoon cinnamon
1 teaspoon ginger
½ teaspoon cloves
½ teaspoon salt
Sugar

Preheat oven to 375 degrees. Lightly grease baking sheets.

In a large bowl, cream together shortening, sugar, molasses and egg until fluffy. Sift together flour, baking soda, cinnamon, ginger, cloves and salt and stir into creamed mixture until well blended. Form dough into 1-inch balls and roll in sugar. Place 2-inches apart on prepared baking sheets and bake 8 to 10 minutes. Cool slightly and remove from baking sheet.

Vernice Roberts

LEBKUCHEN

2 cups brown sugar
4 eggs
¼ cup honey
2½ cups flour
3 tablespoons cocoa powder
2 teaspoons baking powder
1 teaspoon cinnamon
½ teaspoon allspice
¼ teaspoon cloves
⅛ teaspoon salt
½ cup almonds, ground
1 cup sugar
½ cup water

Preheat oven to 350 degrees. Butter and flour a 13x9x3-inch baking pan.

In a large bowl, thoroughly cream the brown sugar and eggs. Beat in the honey until smooth. Sift together the flour, cocoa, baking powder, cinnamon, allspice, cloves and salt. Add to creamed mixture and beat until blended. Stir in almonds. Press dough into prepared pan and bake about 25 minutes.

Combine 1 cup sugar and ½ cup water in a sauce pan and bring to a boil. Pour this syrup over baked Lebkuchen. Cut into squares when almost cool. These keep well in an airtight container.

Gerald W.Frank

SNICKERDOODLES

I am a great-great-great-granddaughter of an Oregon Trail emigrant, Helen Stewart Love, who kept a diary of her arduous journey in 1853.

1 cup shortening
1½ cups sugar
2 eggs
2¾ cups flour
2 teaspoons cream of tartar
1 teaspoon baking soda
½ teaspoon salt
1 tablespoon sugar
2 teaspoons cinnamon

Preheat oven to 400 degrees.

In a large bowl, beat together shortening, 1½ cups sugar and eggs until thoroughly blended. Sift together flour, cream of tartar, baking soda and salt and stir into creamed mixture. Chill dough. In a small dish combine 1 tablespoon sugar and cinnamon.

Roll dough into balls the size of walnuts. Roll in sugar-cinnamon mixture and place on ungreased baking sheets 2-inches apart. Bake for 8 to 10 minutes, or until lightly browned but still soft.

Rindy Ross

SOFT GINGER COOKIES

2 cups molasses
1 cup sugar
1 cup shortening or lard
1 cup buttermilk or sour milk
1 egg
1½ teaspoons ginger
1 teaspoon baking soda
1 teaspoon salt
4½ cups flour

Preheat oven to 350 degrees. Lightly butter cookie sheets.

In a large bowl, combine molasses, sugar, shortening, buttermilk, egg, ginger, baking soda and salt and beat until well blended. Beat in flour to make a stiff dough. Turn out dough onto a lightly floured board and roll out ¼-inch thick. Cut with lightly floured cookie cutter and place on prepared cookie sheets. Bake for 8 to 10 minutes.

Mabel Isabel Distad Whipple
Kit Roberts

GRANDMA WINN'S FRENCH FUDGE

My great-great-grandfather, Thomas Manley Ramsdell, came West in 1844 with the Emigrant Train of 150 Wagons. He settled in Salem, Oregon.

3 cups sugar
⅓ cup light corn syrup
¾ cup milk
1 cup coconut
1 teaspoon vanilla
1 cup nuts, chopped

Oil a 9x9-inch pan.

Combine sugar, corn syrup, milk and coconut in a medium sauce pan. Bring to a boil, stirring constantly. Reduce heat to low, stir and cook slowly until it turns a golden color. When fudge reaches the soft-ball stage, 234 degrees, remove from heat and stir in the vanilla and nuts. Pour into prepared pan and let cool. Cut into squares and store in an airtight container.

Allegra Ramsdell Winn
Dorothy Winn Crawn

TRILBYS

1 cup brown sugar
1 cup butter
½ cup sour milk or buttermilk
1 teaspoon baking soda
2 cups oatmeal
2 cups flour
½ pound pitted dates, minced
1 cup sugar
½ cup water

Preheat oven to 375 degrees. Grease baking sheets.

In a large bowl, cream together the brown sugar and butter until fluffy. Dissolve the baking soda in the sour milk then stir into creamed mixture. Add the oatmeal and flour and beat until well combined. Chill for 1 hour.

Combine the dates, sugar and water in the top of a double-boiler. Cook, stirring often, over simmering water until thick and smooth. Allow date mixture to cool.

Turn dough onto a lightly floured board and roll out ⅛-inch thick. Cut into 2½-inch rounds. Place about 1½ teaspoons of date filling in the center of dough then top with another round. Press edges together with a fork. Bake for about 15 minutes or until edges are browned.

Martha Lunde Hovey
Marilyn Holtorf

WHITE WAFER COOKIES

3 cups flour, sifted
1 teaspoon baking soda
1 teaspoon cream of tartar
1 cup cold butter, cut into small pieces
2 eggs, beaten
1 cup sugar
1 teaspoon vanilla
⅛ teaspoon salt
Sugar for sprinkling

Preheat oven to 350 degrees. Grease baking sheets.

Sift flour, baking soda and cream of tartar into a large bowl. Add cold butter and cut into the flour mixture, like pie dough, until mixture resembles coarse meal. In a separate bowl, beat together eggs, sugar, vanilla and salt until smooth. Add to flour mixture and stir until well combined. Turn dough onto a lightly floured board and roll very thin. Cut into 1-inch shapes and place on prepared baking sheets. Sprinkle with sugar and bake for about 7 minutes. Do not let brown.

Mrs. Adeline Lyons Lee
Marilyn Holtorf

Pies & Pastry

My grandmother was brought to Oregon in the Immigration of 1843 at the age of six. Grandfather arrived in the Immigration of 1847 at age nineteen. Both families settled in the Amity, Oregon area.

In 1852 when William Powell Allen was twenty-four, and Nancy Ann Matheney was fifteen they were married. The age bracket at that time was quite common.

The young couple took a Donation Land Claim high in the mountains north of what is presently Oakridge. Seven children were born. My father, Albert, was the youngest.

When he was a young child, some of Albert's brothers let him come with them, on horseback to Eugene, where he had never been before. Arriving at the big city, the boys tied their horses at a log fence around the city square, near some government buildings. Then Albert saw a strange structure on the far side of the square. He plodded across in very deep mud to investigate with boyish interest. He touched the building. What the heck! Where did they ever find rocks with nice square sides, piled one on top of the other, two floors high?

By this time the brothers had come around and explained that this building was man-made of clay soil baked to a hard consistency.

In later years, Dad entertained us with the story of his discovery of a brick building. There were so many new and strange things out in the world, away from the farm.

Glenn B. Allen

WHITE BEAN PIE

2 cups white beans, soaked overnight,
    then cooked until very tender
½ cup milk
1 cup sugar
2 eggs, well beaten
3 tablespoons butter
½ teaspoon vanilla
Dash nutmeg
1 large unbaked pie shell

Preheat oven to 450 degrees.

Thoroughly mash cooked bean or put through a food processor until smooth. Stir in milk, sugar, eggs, butter, vanilla and nutmeg and blend well. Pour into pie shell. Bake at 450 degrees for 15 minutes. Reduce heat to 325 degrees and bake an additional 30 to 40 minutes or until filling is set.

Helen T. Allen

OLD FASHIONED CREAM PIE

The Osborn family came to Oregon in 1897 by railroad, and settled near other family members who had come to Oregon by wagon train the year earlier.

¾ cup heavy cream
1 cup sugar
6 tablespoons flour
½ cup milk
3 tablespoons butter
One 9-inch unbaked pie shell

Preheat oven to 400 degrees.

In a large bowl, whip cream until stiff. Mix sugar and flour together and fold into whipped cream. Stir in milk and pour into unbaked pie shell. Dot filling with butter. Bake for 30 to 40 minutes, or until filling is set.

Grandma Emma Dorton McCormack Osborn
Marceil Osborn Casselman

MRS. AARON FRANK'S FAVORITE RUM PECAN PIE

3 eggs, beaten
⅔ cup sugar
¼ teaspoon salt
¾ cup corn syrup
¼ cup butter, melted and cooled
¾ cup pecans, chopped
3 ounces rum
One 9-inch unbaked pie shell

Preheat oven to 425 degrees.

In a large bowl, combine eggs, sugar, salt, corn syrup and butter and blend well. Stir in the pecans and rum. Pour into unbaked pie shell and bake for 10 minutes; reduce oven to 350 degrees and bake and additional 35 minutes, or until filling is set.

Don Daniels
Diane Daniels

VINEGAR PIE

The following is truly an Oregon Trail recipe, and a favorite of my grandmother, Mary Elizabeth Linville Davidson, a pioneer of 1846. Since the immigrants had no trees to supply them with fresh fruit, they relied on tomatoes, ground cherries, etc. to make preserves and pies. Vinegar was often used as a substitute for lemon juice.

1 cup sugar
1 tablespoon flour
1 cup cold water
1 egg, lightly beaten
3 tablespoons vinegar
3 tablespoons butter, melted and cooled
Nutmeg to taste
Pastry for a two-crust pie

Preheat oven to 425 degrees.

Stir together sugar and flour in a large bowl. Add water, egg, vinegar, butter and nutmeg and blend well. Pour into unbaked pie shell and top with lattice crust. Bake for 10 minutes, then reduce oven to 350 degrees and continue baking an additional 35 minutes.

Mrs. Morris B. Glickman

LEMON TARTS

These are still a holiday tradition for the descendants of the John and Florence Williams family. They were early settlers of southern Gilliam County, Oregon.

Pie Crust:
3 cups flour
1¼ teaspoons salt
1¼ cups shortening
5 tablespoons water
1 teaspoon vinegar
1 egg

Filling:
½ cup butter
2 cups sugar
⅔ cup lemon juice
Zest of 2 lemons, finely minced
6 eggs, well beaten

Preheat oven to 400 degrees.

Sift together flour and salt into a large bowl. Cut in shortening until mixture resembles coarse meal. In a small bowl, stir water, vinegar and egg with a fork. Pour over flour mixture and stir together just until ingredients are moistened and hold together. Turn out dough onto a lightly floured board and roll out. Cut with a biscuit cutter or glass that is ½-inch larger than the bottom of miniature muffin pan cup. Fit dough in the miniature muffin pans. Chill until needed.

Melt butter in top of double-boiler. Add sugar, lemon juice, lemon zest and eggs and whisk constantly until the thickness of honey. Pour 1½ teaspoons of filling into prepared tart shells and bake for 10 to 15 minutes. Makes about 8 dozen.

Marie McCarty

LEMON SOUR CREAM PIE

⅔ cup sugar
3 tablespoons corn starch
1 cup milk
3 egg yolks
¼ cup lemon juice
1 teaspoon lemon zest, finely minced
¼ cup butter
1 cup sour cream
1 9-inch baked pie shell
Whipped cream

Mix sugar and cornstarch together in a heavy sauce pan. Whisk in milk until smooth, then egg yolks until well blended. Stir in lemon juice, lemon zest and butter. Place on medium heat and cook, whisking constantly, for 4 to 5 minutes. Do not let boil. When thickened, remove from heat and cool to room temperature. Stir in sour cream until well blended. Pour filling into baked pie shell. Cover and chill at least 6 hours before serving. Serve with whipped cream.

Mary Peters

GRANDMA SCHWEISS'S RHUBARB PIE

3½ cups rhubarb, cut into 1-inch pieces
1¼ cups sugar
6 tablespoons flour
1 egg, slightly beaten
Pastry for a 2-crust pie

Preheat oven to 425 degrees.
Line a pie pan with pastry and chill until needed. Combine rhubarb, sugar, flour and egg and mix well. Pour into prepared pie pan and top with a lattice crust. Bake for 40 to 45 minutes.

Betsy Krause

ELIZA OLIVER'S CHESS TARTS

My husband's grandmother, Eliza Oliver, used to make Chess Tarts for her husband, Herman Oliver, and their guests who visited the Oliver Ranch in John Day, Oregon. Her mother, Grandma Lawrence, taught her how to make them.

1 cup sugar
1 whole egg
2 egg yolks
1 cup seedless raisins,
    either white or dark
¾ cup walnuts, chopped
½ cup butter, melted
Pastry for a single-crust pie
2 egg whites
4 tablespoons sugar

Preheat oven to 450 degrees. Press pastry into muffin tins and chill until ready to use.
Beat sugar into whole egg and 2 egg yolks until light. Stir in raisins, walnuts and butter until well blended. Pour filling into prepared pastry in muffin tins. Bake for 15 minutes.
Beat 2 egg whites until stiff, gradually adding 4 tablespoons of sugar. Pie lightly on baked tarts. Reduce heat to 325 degrees and bake tarts an additional 15 minutes.

Mrs. Oliver Keerins

BLUEBERRY PIE

1 cup sour cream
¾ cup sugar
1 egg, slightly beaten
1 teaspoon salt
2 cups blueberries
1 unbaked pie shell
3 tablespoons nuts, finely chopped
3 tablespoons flour
1 tablespoon butter

Preheat oven to 400 degrees.

In a large bowl, combine sour cream, sugar, egg and salt and beat with an electric mixer for 5 minutes. Fold in blueberries and pour into unbaked pie shell. Bake for 25 minutes. Combine nuts, flour and butter and sprinkle on top of pie. Bake an additional 10 minutes. Chill before serving.

Pie Crust:

3 cups flour
1¼ cups shortening
1 egg, beaten
5 tablespoons cold water
1 tablespoon vinegar
1 teaspoon salt

In a large bowl, cut shortening into flour until it resembles coarse meal. Combine egg, water, vinegar and salt and pour into flour mixture. Stir gently until just moistened, do not overmix. Turn out dough onto lightly floured board. Roll out dough and fit into pie plate. Chill until ready to use.

Tammy Lindahl

VINEGAR PIE FILLING

My great-great-great-grandparents, Nicholas and Delilah Shrum, came west in 1846 with the Orus Brown Wagon Train. Their Donation Land Claim spread up the rolling hills east of present day Salem, Oregon. There, in a stand of tall fir trees, they built their home. The white, two-story house still stands facing west towards the Willamette River.

1 cup sugar
3 egg yolks, beaten
4 tablespoons vinegar
3 tablespoons flour
1 teaspoon lemon extract
⅛ teaspoon salt
1½ cups boiling water
3 egg whites
1 tablespoon sugar
1 baked pie shell

Preheat oven to 350 degrees.

Combine 1 cup sugar, egg yolks, vinegar, flour, lemon extract and salt in the top of a double boiler over simmering water. Slowly whisk in the boiling water, and cook, stirring constantly, until thick. Cool filling slightly and pour into baked pie shell.

Beat egg whites until they form soft peaks. Sprinkle 1 tablespoon sugar over egg whites, and continue beating until stiff. Spread over pie filling, sealing to the crust. Bake for about 10 minutes or until topping is golden brown.

Lucile Fidler

STRAWBERRY RHUBARB PIE

¾ cup sugar
⅓ cup cornstarch
1 teaspoon salt
4 cups milk
5 egg yolks, slightly beaten
3 tablespoons butter, softened
1 teaspoon vanilla
Two 9-inch pie shells, baked
3 cups strawberries, halved
3 cups rhubarb, thinly sliced
½ teaspoon orange zest, finely chopped
1½ cups sugar
5 to 6 tablespoons cornstarch

Stir together ¾ cup sugar, ⅓ cup cornstarch and salt in a heavy saucepan. Blend milk and egg yolks together and gradually add to sugar mixture, whisking constantly. Cook over medium heat, stirring constantly, until mixture begins to thicken. Bring to a boil, stirring constantly, for 1 minute. Remove from heat and stir in butter and vanilla. Immediately pour into baked pie shells. Cover with plastic wrap, pressing onto filling. Chill 1 hour.

Combine strawberries, rhubarb and orange zest in a large saucepan. Combine 1½ cups sugar with 5 to 6 tablespoons cornstarch and stir into fruit. Cook over medium-low heat until thickened and clear, stirring constantly. Remove from heat and let cool for 30 minutes. Gently pour over custard pie filling. Chill for at least 2 hours before serving.

Shirley Curry

"PIE CRUST DELICATE AND TENDER"

2 cups flour
1 cup shortening
1 teaspoon salt
¼ cup ice water

Cut the flour and shortening together until it resembles coarse meal. Dissolve the salt in the ice water and add to flour mixture. Stir just until dough is moistened and comes together, do not over mix. Divide dough in 2 pieces and chill until ready to use.

Louise Sieler Stupperich
Marion Krause
Betsy Krause

Nathaniel Green McDonald and his wife, Rebecca Jane McDonald were Oregon Trail pioneers of 1846. They took up a Donation Land Claim northwest of Scio, Oregon near Shelburn. He built and operated the first ferry on the North Santiam River. The following story was passed down through the family:

In the 1850's, Mrs. McDonald took wool the family had sheared, washed, carded, dyed, spun into yarn, and made into wool cloth. She then made wool suits for two of her young sons. The boys were in the 8-12 year old range.

The family received word of a wagon train coming to use the ferry and on it were some friends from the East. Mrs. McDonald dressed her boys in their new suits and sent them to meet the wagon train and tell their friends how to get to their home. When their friends arrived, Mrs. McDonald asked them if her boys had directed them. They said no, but the two of the cutest little Indian boys, all clad in buckskins, had told them. One can imagine the uproar when she discovered the boys had traded clothes with the Indian boys!

Lynda Hatch and Marley Sims

Dried Apple Pie

Soak 2 cups dried apples in water overnight. Drain off the water and mix apples with ½ cup sugar and one teaspoon each of allspice and cinnamon. Line an 8-inch pie pan with a crust, add the apple mixture, dot with 3 tablespoons of butter and cover with a second crust. Make a few slashes in the top for ventilation and bake in a 350 degree oven for about one hour, or until the crust is golden brown.

Lynda Hatch

RHUBARB CUSTARD PIE

2½ cups rhubarb, cut into 1-inch pieces
1½ cups sugar
¼ cup flour
2 eggs, lightly beaten
2 teaspoons lemon juice
Dash of salt
2 tablespoons butter
1 tablespoon sugar
Pastry for a double-crust pie

Preheat oven to 450 degrees.

Combine rhubarb, sugar, flour, eggs, lemon juice, and salt in a large bowl and toss together well. Line a pie plate with pastry. Fill with rhubarb mixture and dot with butter. Adjust top crust and sprinkle with 1 tablespoon sugar. Bake at 450 degrees for 10 minutes, then reduce heat to 350 degrees and continue to bake an additional 30 minutes.

Juanita Boyk

GRANDMA OSIE'S RAISIN PIE

Gram Bates married a man who drove cattle all the way to the gold mines in California. This left her alone one winter in a small cabin in the Colorado Springs area. One afternoon the cabin was knocked off its foundations by fighting buffalo! She had one daughter, Osa Bates, who made wonderful Raisin Pie.

2 cups raisins, rinsed and drained
2 cups water
¾ cup sugar
2 tablespoons cornstarch
2 tablespoons butter
1 tablespoon vinegar
½ teaspoon salt
½ cup chopped walnuts (optional)
Pastry for a 2-crust pie
Milk

Preheat oven to 425 degrees.

Combine raisins and water in a large sauce pan. Stir the sugar and cornstarch together then blend into the raisin mixture. Stir in the butter, vinegar, salt and walnuts. Bring to a boil, stirring constantly, and boil for 2 minutes. Pour into pastry shell and top with a lattice crust. Brush lattice top with a little milk. Bake for 15 minutes, then lower heat to 350 degrees and continue to bake for an additional 35 minutes.

Jacqueline Mitchael

JUICY APPLE CRISP

2 pounds Jonathan apples; peeled,
    cored and thinly sliced
¼ cup sugar
6 tablespoons flour
1½ teaspoons cinnamon
½ cup brown sugar, firmly packed
¼ teaspoon nutmeg
6 tablespoons butter
¾ cup quick-cooking oatmeal
Evaporated milk or whipping cream
    as an accompaniment

Preheat oven to 350 degrees. Generously butter a 9x9 inch baking dish.

Place sliced apples in a large mixing bowl. Combine sugar, 1 tablespoon flour and ½ teaspoon cinnamon; pour over apples and toss to coat. Pour into prepared baking dish.

Put remaining flour, remaining cinnamon, brown sugar and nutmeg in bowl. Lightly work in the butter with a fork just until crumbly. Stir in oatmeal and spread over the apples making sure edges are covered. Bake 40 to 45 minutes or until apples are tender. Serve with evaporated milk or whipping cream.

Mrs. Jacquie Young

In 1845, eleven of the King children, four with their own families, made the westward trek with their parents, Nahum and Serepta King. There were 26 of them when they left Missouri. One man, two women, a three year old girl and a baby boy died during the trip. Sarah King Chambers died of what was called "camp fever" on the Meek Cutoff in the Malheur Mountains. The others died when a raft overturned in the Columbia River.

The group spent the first Oregon winter at Gales Creek near Forest Grove, Oregon. The men went land-hunting, and in the spring, the families moved to the provisional land claims that they had staked out. This area came to be known as Kings Valley.

Lucius and Hopestill (King) Norton were parents of the first white child born in Kings Valley, in 1847. Her name was Ashnah, and she was my great-grandmother. Ashnah was 17 years old when she married Private James Plunkett, a gunner and part-time drummer at Fort Hoskins. After his discharge, they also settled in Kings Valley.

My grandmother, Mrs. Bertha (Plunkett) Thompson, made the most wonderful Pear Pie, and I have copied it as she wrote it.

Pear Pie

The pear pie is hard to tell you, because most of it, I guess at. Cut your pears in small pieces, only have a bottom crust, no top. Have enough pears for a medium thick pie. Sweeten then mix a little flour through the pears with the sugar to thicken the juice. Then put in a crust with a little cinnamon over the top and quite a bit of good cream and a few small pieces of butter around over the top of pears. Bake till pears are good and done. Pears must be good and soft and ripe.

(My grandmother added this note to the recipe, "I hope that you can get this in your noodle so you can have a good pie.")

Nadine Long

APPLE TART FROM FORT VANCOUVER

Pastry:

    5 cups flour
    6 teaspoons baking powder
    1 teaspoon salt
    ½ cup butter
    2 cups light cream

Sift together dry ingredients into a large bowl. With a pastry cutter, cut in butter until mixture resembles coarse meal. Stir in cream then turn out dough onto lightly floured board. Knead gently, then chill while filling is prepared.

Filling:

    8 tart apples
    Juice of 1 lemon
    1½ cups sugar
    1 teaspoon cinnamon
    ½ cup currants
    ¼ cup butter
    Sweetened cream as an accompaniment

Preheat oven to 450 degrees. Generously butter a 2-quart baking dish.

Pare, core and slice apples. Sprinkle lemon juice over apples. Stir sugar and cinnamon together then toss with apples. Add currants and toss together. Put mixture in buttered baking dish and dot all over with the ¼ cup of butter. Roll out pastry on a lightly floured board to ½-inch thick. Cover the top of the dish with the pastry and seal to the edge of the dish. Crimp edges decoratively. Cut two or three steam vents on top and sprinkle with a little additional sugar if desired. Bake for 10 minutes, then reduce heat to 350 degrees and continue to bake for 30 minutes more. Serve with sweetened cream.

Rick Edwards
Park Ranger
Fort Vancouver National Historic Site

PEACH COBBLER

    6 peaches, peeled and sliced
    1 cup sugar
    ¾ cup flour
    ½ cup sugar
    2 teaspoons baking powder
    ⅛ teaspoon salt
    ¾ cup milk
    1 cup butter, melted
    Cream

Preheat oven to 350 degrees.

Combine peaches and 1 cup sugar and set aside for 10 minutes. In a large bowl, stir together the flour, ½ cup sugar, baking powder and salt. Pour in milk and stir until smooth. Pour melted butter into a 13x9-inch baking dish. Pour in batter over melted butter, then put peaches on top. Bake for about 1 hour. Serve with cream.

Vernice Roberts

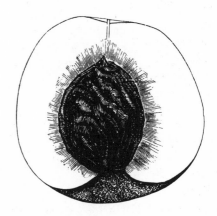

LEMON CHEESE FILLING

    6 eggs, beaten well
    2 cups sugar
    ½ cup lemon juice
    Zest of 2 lemons
    2 tablespoons butter

Combine all ingredients in the top of a double boiler. Cook over simmering water, whisking constantly, until thick. Cool and use on cake or in baked tart shells.

Marie High

GREAT-GRANDMOTHER HOVEY'S PUMPKIN PIE AND CRUST

Filling
    2 cups milk, warmed
    2 cups brown sugar
    2 cups pumpkin, cooked or canned
    4 eggs, lightly beaten
    2 teaspoons cinnamon
    1 teaspoon ginger

Preheat oven to 450 degrees.

Combine all ingredients in a large bowl and stir until well blended and smooth. Pour into unbaked pie shell. Bake at 450 degrees for 10 minutes then reduce temperature to 325 degrees and bake an additional 40 minutes.

Pie Crust
    5 cups flour
    1 cup butter
    1 cup shortening
    ½ cup cold water
    1 egg
    1 tablespoon lemon juice
    1 tablespoon sugar
    1¼ teaspoons baking powder
    1 teaspoon salt

In a large bowl combine flour, butter and shortening until mixture resembles oatmeal. In a separate bowl combine remaining ingredients and stir with fork until smooth.

Pour liquid over flour mixture and stir gently until just moistened. Do not overmix. Gather dough into ball and divide into thirds. Gently flatten into discs. Cover and chill to make rolling easier. Makes enough dough for one double-crust pie and one single-crust pie.

Martha Lunde Hovey

SOUR CREAM PIE

This is a recipe that belonged to my Grandmother, Mary Elizabeth Gibbins Miller, who came to Oregon from Missouri in 1852. She and her husband settled at Providence where they raised a family of ten children. As far as I know this recipe probably came with them.

    1 cup brown sugar
    2 egg yolks
    1 cup sour cream
    1 teaspoon nutmeg
    1 teaspoon cinnamon
    1 cup raisins, chopped
    2 egg whites
    1 unbaked pie shell

Preheat oven to 425 degrees.

Combine brown sugar and egg yolks in a large mixing bowl and beat well. Stir in sour cream, nutmeg, cinnamon and raisins until smooth. In a separate bowl, beat egg whites until stiff then gently fold into sour cream mixture. Pour into pie shell and bake for 15 minutes. Lower the heat to 350 degrees and continue to bake for approximately 40 minutes, or until filling is set.

Lela Miller Jacklin

POORMAN'S PECAN PIE

During the depression you had to make do with what you had on hand. In the later years walnuts were added to the recipe.

    1 cup brown sugar
    1 cup oatmeal
    1 cup corn syrup
    ½ cup margarine
    2 eggs
    1 unbaked pie shell

Preheat oven to 350 degrees.

Combine all ingredients and blend well. Pour into pie shell and bake 45 to 50 minutes.

Janice M. Hardy

BROWN BETTY

2 apples; peeled, cored and diced
1 cup bread crumbs, in all
½ cup sugar
¼ teaspoon nutmeg
⅛ teaspoon salt
3 tablespoons melted butter
3 tablespoons water

Preheat oven to 350 degrees. Butter an 8x8-inch baking pan.

Combine apples, ¾ cup bread crumbs, sugar, nutmeg and salt and toss together to mix. Put into prepared pan. Sprinkle remaining ¼ cup bread crumbs on top of apple mixture. Sprinkle butter and water over top. Cover with a lid or with foil and bake for 15 minutes, then uncover and bake an additional 30 minutes.

Ethel Wiggins Reynolds
Jane Reynolds Hyatt
Mary Westmorland

SPRITZ GEBACKENES

1 cup milk
2 tablespoons water
½ cup butter
1¾ cups flour
5 to 6 eggs

Preheat oven to 400 degrees. Lightly grease baking sheets.

In a sauce pan, combine milk, water and butter and bring to a boil. Take pan off the heat and stir in the flour all at once, it will pull away from the sides and form a mass. Beat in the eggs one at a time, beating well after each addition. Fill a pastry bag and pipe out 1-inch mounds on baking sheets. Bake 15 to 20 minutes or until golden brown and they have doubled in size. These can be filled with sweetened whipped cream, custard or ice cream.

Gerald W. Frank

STRAWBERRY CRUMBLE

¾ cup slivered almonds, finely chopped
¾ cup dry, unseasoned breadcrumbs
½ cup brown sugar
⅛ teaspoon cinnamon
⅛ teaspoon nutmeg
1 pound strawberries, hulled and halved
4 tablespoons butter, softened

Preheat oven to 350 degrees. Grease a 9x9-inch pan.

Combine almonds, breadcrumbs, brown sugar, cinnamon, and nutmeg and stir to mix. Take half of this mixture and toss together with the strawberries. Put strawberry mixture into the prepared pan. Add butter to the remaining crumb mixture and stir to blend. Spread evenly over strawberries. Bake for about 20 minutes. Allow to stand 10 minutes before serving.

Virginia A. Whipple

Puddings & Dumplings

GRANDMA MEACHAM'S RHUBARB PUDDING

My grandparents, Alfred B. Meacham and Orpha Ferree Meacham, settled in the Blue Mountains of Oregon around the middle of the 1800s. Alfred Meacham was the Commissioner of Indian Affairs for Oregon. He was scalped by Indians and survived to take a small group of Indians back East where he gave talks at colleges and assemblies on how we had wronged the Indians. Orpha Meacham was hostess to traders that came West and was noted for her delicious food.

1 pound rhubarb, cut into 1-inch pieces
3 tablespoons brown sugar
2 cups flour
1 cup sugar
2½ teaspoons baking powder
1 teaspoon salt
½ cup milk
1 tablespoon oil
1 egg, lightly beaten
Butter
Brown sugar

Preheat oven to 350 degrees. Butter a 13x9-inch baking dish.

Combine rhubarb and 3 tablespoons brown sugar and spread in baking dish. In a large bowl, combine flour, sugar, baking powder, salt, milk, oil and egg and beat until smooth. Pour batter over rhubarb and bake for 30 to 40 minutes, or until golden brown. Serve hot, spread with butter and sprinkled with brown sugar.

Elizabeth Redington Meacham Stewart

BROWN SUGAR DUMPLINGS

6 tablespoons sugar
6 tablespoons shortening
2 cups flour
4 teaspoons baking powder
¼ teaspoon salt
1 cup milk
1 teaspoon vanilla
2 cups water
2 cups brown sugar
4 tablespoons butter

In a large bowl, cream together the sugar and shortening. Sift the flour, baking powder and salt together and add to the creamed mixture. Add the milk and vanilla and beat until smooth.

Combine the water, brown sugar and butter in a large pot and bring to a boil. Cook for 5 minutes. Reduce heat to low and drop dumplings by the tablespoonful into the syrup. Cover pot and simmer for 15 minutes. Serve hot.

Vera Merwin Schneider Botorf

Apple Treat

Line the bottom of a pudding dish with buttered bread and cover with sweetened applesauce. Repeat till half full, bread on top. Then mix 2 eggs, 1 pint milk, ½ cup sugar and ½ teaspoon salt. Pour over bread and applesauce. Bake until set. Serve cold with cream, sugar and nutmeg gratings or cinnamon.

Lynda Hatch

LEMON CUSTARD PUDDING

My great-great-grandmother, Mary Elizabeth Boone Norris, was a great-granddaughter of Daniel Boone. She came to Oregon in 1846, with her husband, Thomas Norris, her father, Alphonso Boone, and her brothers and sisters. Her older sister, Chloe, married George Law Curry, territorial governor of Oregon.

1 cup sugar
1 tablespoon butter
2 eggs, separated
1 cup milk
1 cup flour
Juice of 1 lemon
Zest of 1 lemon, finely minced

Preheat oven to 350 degrees.

In a large bowl, cream the sugar and butter together. Beat in the egg yolks, one at a time, beating well after each addition. Add the milk, flour, lemon juice and lemon zest and beat well. In a separate bowl, beat egg whites until stiff. Carefully fold into the batter. Pour into a 1½-quart baking dish and set it in a pan of hot water that comes halfway up the sides of the dish. Bake for about 50 to 60 minutes. Do not let it get too brown on top.

Aileen Barker Rickard

SON-OF-A-GUN-IN-A-SACK

When the ranch cook wanted to be especially nice to the cowhands, he made a boiled pudding sometimes called Son-of-a-Gun-in-a-Sack. Raisins or dried apples and suet were added to a soft dough. Following the old colonial method, the mass was placed in a cloth sack and boiled in a big kettle of water until done. Perhaps it got its name because it was so much trouble to make.

2 cups flour
1½ cups soft bread crumbs
½ cup brown sugar, packed
1 tablespoon baking soda
1 teaspoon salt
1 teaspoon cinnamon
¼ teaspoon ground cloves
¼ teaspoon nutmeg
1 cup raisins
1 cup suet, ground
½ cup nuts, chopped
⅔ cup evaporated milk
½ cup light molasses
Sweetened whipped cream (optional)

In mixing bowl combine flour, bread crumbs, sugar, soda, salt, cinnamon, cloves, and nutmeg. Stir in raisins, suet, and nuts. Stir in milk and molasses; mix well. Arrange layers of cheesecloth to form a 16-inch square about ⅛-inch thick; set in a 1-quart bowl. Fill cheesecloth with pudding mixture; bring up sides of cheesecloth allowing room for expansion of the pudding; tie tightly with string. Place the "sack" in a colander. Place colander in kettle; add enough boiling water to cover the sack. Cover; boil gently for two hours. Remove colander from pan; remove cheesecloth from around pudding at once. Turn pudding, rounded side up, on plate. Let stand 30 minutes before serving. Serve warm with whipped cream, if desired. Serves 10 to 12 people.

Lynda Hatch

GOOSEBERRY DUMPLINGS

My mother, Erma Smith Shelburne, spoke proudly when she told of her "people" coming west on the wagon trains in 1843, 1845, 1847 and 1863. Her great-grandfather, Henry Hewitt, drove the first wagon down the west slope of the Blue Mountains during the Great Migration of 1843.

4 cups flour
6 teaspoons baking powder
2 teaspoons salt
2 cups whipping cream
4 cups whole gooseberries
4 cups whipping cream
1½ cups sugar
1 teaspoon allspice
1 teaspoon cinnamon
1 teaspoon nutmeg

Sift together the flour, baking powder and salt into a large bowl and make a well in the center. Pour the 2 cups of cream into the well all at once. Stir until the dough comes away from the sides of the bowl. Turn the dough out onto a lightly floured board and knead lightly, 8 to 10 folds. Roll out ¼-inch thick. Cut into 8 squares and place about ½ cup of gooseberries in the center of the dough. Bring up the edges of the dough to completely enclose the gooseberries, pinch together to seal. Place dumplings in the top of a steamer, and steam over simmering water for about 20 minutes.

To make the sauce, combine 4 cups cream, 1½ cups sugar, allspice, cinnamon and nutmeg in a medium saucepan. Simmer over low heat until sugar dissolves. Serve over warm dumplings. Oh-so-good!

Dina Nuxoll

BREAD PUDDING WITH BRANDY SAUCE

4 slices homemade style bread, cubed
⅓ cup brown sugar
½ teaspoon cinnamon
⅓ cup raisins
2 tablespoons butter, melted
2½ cups milk
3 eggs, slightly beaten
⅓ cup sugar
1 teaspoon vanilla
⅛ teaspoon salt

Preheat oven to 350 degrees. Butter a 9x9-inch pan.

Put bread cubes in prepared pan and lightly toast in the oven for about 10 to 12 minutes. Remove from oven. Stir together the brown sugar and cinnamon and sprinkle over the toasted bread cubes. Sprinkle the raisins and melted butter over bread. In a medium bowl, combine milk, eggs, sugar, vanilla and salt and blend well. Pour mixture over bread mixture. Bake for 60 to 70 minutes, or until pudding is set. Serve warm with Brandy Sauce or whipped cream.

Brandy Sauce

1 cup whipping cream
1 cup brown sugar
¼ cup butter
¼ cup brandy

Combine whipping cream, brown sugar and butter in a heavy sauce pan. Bring to a boil, stirring constantly. Remove from heat and stir in brandy, beat until smooth.

Virginia A. Whipple

LEMON PUDDING

My great-grandfather, Charles Peter Bailey, was nine years old when he came across the Oregon Trail from Missouri in 1852. He later became a Baptist minister and Circuit Rider, making his way by horseback wherever he was needed.

1 cup sugar
5 tablespoons flour
3 tablespoons butter, melted
3 eggs, separated
1 cup milk
½ cup orange juice
1 tablespoon lemon juice

Preheat oven to 350 degrees.

Sift the sugar and flour into a large bowl. Beat in the butter and egg yolks until light. Add the milk, orange juice and lemon juice and mix well. Beat the egg whites until they hold soft peaks then fold into the batter. Pour batter into a 1½-quart baking dish and set it in a pan of hot water that comes halfway up the sides of the dish. Bake for 50 to 60 minutes, don't let it get too brown. Let cool and serve at room temperature or chilled.

Cynthia Berne

IRISH POTATO PUDDING

1 pound potatoes, cooked and mashed
2 cups sugar
2 cups butter, well creamed
5 eggs, beaten
½ cup whipping cream
¼ cup brandy

Preheat oven to 350 degrees. Generously butter a 2-quart baking dish.

Combine all ingredients and beat until smooth. Pour into prepared baking dish and bake for about 1 hour.

Irene Akerson

BREAD PUDDING WITH LEMON SAUCE

4 eggs
1½ cups sugar
6 tablespoons butter, melted
1½ teaspoons nutmeg
1½ teaspoons cinnamon
½ teaspoon vanilla
3 cups milk
¾ cup raisins
¾ cup toasted pecans, chopped
5 cups stale bread, cubed
5 cups stale cake, croissants, muffins
    or other; cubed

Preheat oven to 300 degrees. Butter a 13x9 inch-baking dish very well.

In a large mixing bowl beat eggs until light and fluffy. Add sugar, butter, nutmeg, cinnamon and vanilla. Beat until well blended and sugar is dissolved. Stir in 2 cups of the milk, raisins and pecans until thoroughly combined. Place bread cubes and cake cubes in prepared baking dish. Pour over egg mixture and toss lightly until bread is soaked. Let stand about 10 minutes, gently patting bread down into liquid occasionally. Pour enough of the remaining milk over mixture to insure bread is submerged in liquid. Cover with foil and set dish in a larger pan of hot water. Bake for 1½ hours or until set in the center. Serve with Lemon Sauce.

Lemon Sauce
1 cup water
¾ cup sugar
Half of a lemon
2 tablespoons cornstarch
¼ cup cold water
¾ teaspoon vanilla
Juice of 1 large lemon

Combine 1 cup water, sugar and lemon half in a saucepan. Bring to a boil. Dissolve cornstarch with ¼ cup cold water and whisk into boiling mixture. Reduce heat to medium and cook, stirring constantly, until slightly thickened. Whisk in vanilla and lemon juice. Remove from heat and strain sauce into sauce boat. Serve warm.

Mrs. Jacquie Young

MOLASSES PUDDING

1 cup molasses
1 cup buttermilk
¼ cup butter
¼ cup lard, (or shortening)
3 eggs, beaten
2 cups flour
1 teaspoon baking soda

Preheat oven to 350 degrees. Generously butter a 2-quart baking dish.
Combine all ingredients and beat until smooth. Pour into prepared baking dish and bake for about 1 hour.

Irene Akerson

CHOCOLATE BREAD PUDDING

1½ cups milk
1 cup soft bread crumbs
3 tablespoons cocoa
½ cup sugar
⅛ teaspoon salt
2 eggs, separated
½ cup coconut
1 teaspoon vanilla

Preheat oven to 350 degrees and grease baking dish.
Scald milk and pour 1¼ cups over bread crumbs, let stand 5 minutes. Stir cocoa, sugar and salt together then add remaining ¼ cup of hot milk and blend well. Stir into bread crumb mixture. Beat egg yolks until light then stir in coconut and vanilla. Add to bread crumb mixture. Beat egg whites until stiff and fold into mixture gently. Pour into greased dish and bake until firm.

Araminta Phillips
Daralene Wade

VIRGINIA BARROW'S CARROT PUDDING

1 cup potato, grated
1 cup carrot, grated
1 cup raisins
1 cup sugar
1 cup flour
1 teaspoon baking soda
1 teaspoon cloves
1 teaspoon cinnamon
1 teaspoon allspice
1 tablespoon butter

Butter a 2-quart pudding mold.
In a large bowl, combine all ingredients and mix until smooth. Pour batter into mold until two-thirds full and cover tightly with lid. Steam for 3 hours.

Daralene Wade

OSARK APPLE PUDDING

Petra Beiber came to the West from Nebraska, her parents were Danish. She and her husband George settled in the Medical Springs area of Baker County and raised cattle. I am her daughter, also a rancher.

  2 eggs, beaten
  1½ cups sugar
  ½ cup flour
  2½ teaspoons baking powder
  ¼ teaspoon salt
  1 cup apples, coarsely chopped
  1 cup nuts, chopped

Preheat oven to 325 degrees. Grease a 9x9x2-inch pan.

In a mixing bowl, beat eggs and sugar together until light and fluffy. Sift together flour, baking powder and salt and stir into egg mixture. Add apples and nuts and stir until smooth. Pour into prepared pan and bake for approximately 25 minutes.

Eloise Colton

DUMMLINGS

DUMPLINGS

On the Trail from Missouri to Oregon in 1853, my great-grandmother, Mary Henderson Howard Birks, would sometimes be fortunate enough to come upon a patch of wild gooseberries, blackberries or a wild apple, plum or cherry tree. Knowing there was a treat in store from his newlywed bride, Jeremiah Birks would pause long enough to allow her to pick the fruit. That evening my great-grandmother would serve this dessert wherever her kitchen would be.

  1 quart fruit; peeled, seeded and chopped
  1 cup flour
  1½ teaspoons baking powder
  Pinch of salt
  1 egg
  ¼ cup milk, approximately

Put fruit in a medium sauce pan and simmer over medium heat. When fruit is cooked, add enough water to make 1 quart of fruit and juice. Bring to a simmer.

Sift dry ingredients into a bowl. Put egg in a measuring cup and add milk until it measures ½ cup. Stir the egg and milk together with a fork. Stir into flour mixture until it forms a stiff batter.

Drop the batter from a tablespoon into the simmering fruit. Continue until all batter is used. Cover and cook over low heat for 20 minutes.

Donnabelle James Robanske

GRANDMA HUBBARD'S TOP OF THE STOVE RICE PUDDING

Grandma Hubbard was born Mary Clara DeGuire September 28, 1848 in Fredricktown, Madison, Missouri to Francois and Elenore St. Gemme DeGuire. The DeGuires crossed the plains in 1854 going the first year to the area near Marysville, California. In the spring of 1855 they came to the French Prairie area of the Willamette Valley. Mary Clara married David Riley Hubbard on September 16, 1866 in Silverton, Oregon. He was the son of Joseph Hubbard and Sarah E. Venable who had crossed the plains in 1853 from Pike County, Illinois. The Joseph Hubbard family settled a Donation Land Claim in the Silverton Hills. The town of Hubbard, Oregon was named after Joseph's older brother Charles, a pioneer of 1847.

½ cup water
¼ cup rice
1 cup milk
½ teaspoon vanilla
¼ cup sugar
1 egg, separated
1 tablespoon cornstarch
1 tablespoon butter
½ cup raisins (optional)
⅛ teaspoon cream of tartar
1 tablespoon sugar

In a saucepan bring water to a boil, stir in rice with a fork and bring back to a boil. Reduce heat to low, cover and simmer for about 20 minutes or until water is absorbed and rice is tender. In a heavy saucepan, bring the milk, vanilla and half the sugar to a boil. In a bowl, beat the egg yolk with the remaining sugar until foamy then beat in the cornstarch. Dilute this mixture with half of the hot milk, whisking, then pour back into the saucepan and cook over low heat, until mixture thickens, whisking constantly. Whisk in the butter until smooth. Stir in the rice and raisins if desired. Beat egg white until foamy then add cream of tartar and beat until soft peaks. Beat in 1 tablespoon sugar until stiff. Spread meringue over pudding and place in oven under broiler until golden brown.

Clara M. Foster

MRS. EMIL FRANK EM'S CHOCOLATE PUDDING

2 cups milk
1 cup zwieback cracker crumbs
¾ cup semi-sweet chocolate, chopped
6 eggs, separated
6 tablespoons sugar
Whipped Cream

Butter 2-quart pudding mold.

Combine milk and zwieback crumbs in a sauce pan and simmer until thickened. Remove from heat and stir in chocolate, allow to cool. In a large bowl, beat egg yolks until light, then add sugar and beat until very thick. Stir into chocolate mixture. Beat egg whites until stiff then fold into batter. Pour batter into prepared mold, cover tightly with lid, and steam 1½ hours.

Unmold onto serving dish and garnish with whipped cream.

Gerald W. Frank

STEAMED PUDDING WITH PLAIN SAUCE

This recipe is from my great-grandmother, Anna Pence, who came to live near the Snake River near Payette, Idaho in 1840.

1 cup molasses
1 cup warm water
1 egg, beaten
2½ cups flour
1 teaspoon baking soda
1 cup raisins

In a large bowl, blend molasses and water. Stir in the egg. Add the flour and baking soda and beat until smooth. Stir in raisins. Pour batter into a greased 2-quart pudding mold two-thirds full. Cover with lid tightly and steam 2½ hours. Serve with Plain Sauce.

Plain Sauce
1 cup brown sugar
1 tablespoon flour
⅛ teaspoon salt
1 cup fruit juice or water
3 tablespoons butter
½ teaspoon vanilla

In a sauce pan combine brown sugar, flour, salt and fruit juice and bring to a boil. Reduce heat to medium and cook for 10 minutes. Stir in butter and vanilla. Serve hot.

Marcia Gray

SUNBURST APPLE DUMPLINGS

1½ cups sugar
1½ cups water
¼ teaspoon cinnamon
¼ teaspoon nutmeg
10 drops red food coloring
3 tablespoons butter
2 cups flour
2 teaspoons baking powder
1 teaspoon salt
⅔ cup shortening
½ cup milk
6 medium apples, peeled and cored
6 teaspoons butter
2 tablespoons sugar
1 teaspoon cinnamon
¼ teaspoon nutmeg

Preheat oven to 375 degrees. Lightly butter a 14x10-inch baking dish.

In a sauce pan, combine 1½ cups sugar, water, ¼ teaspoon cinnamon, ¼ teaspoon nutmeg and food coloring and bring to a boil. Stir in 3 tablespoons butter, remove from heat, and set aside.

Sift together flour, baking powder and salt into a large bowl. Cut in shortening until it resembles coarse meal. Pour in milk all at once, and stir just to moisten. Turn out onto lightly floured board and roll dough ⅛-inch thick. Cut into six 6-inch squares, and place an apple on each square. Put 1 teaspoon of butter on each apple. Combine 2 tablespoons sugar, 1 teaspoon cinnamon and ¼ teaspoon nutmeg and sprinkle over apples. Moisten edges of dough and pinch together to enclose each apple. Prick tops with sunburst pattern and place 1-inch apart in prepared baking dish. Pour reserved syrup over dumplings, and bake for about 35 minutes.

Kit Roberts

UPSIDE DOWN CHOCOLATE PUDDING

This pudding makes its own sauce.

1 cup flour
¾ cup sugar
3 tablespoons cocoa powder
2 teaspoons baking powder
½ teaspoon salt
½ cup milk
1 teaspoon vanilla
2 tablespoons oil
½ cup nuts, chopped
1¼ cups sugar
¼ cup cocoa powder
2 cups hot water

Preheat oven to 350 degrees. Butter an 8x8x2-inch cake pan.

Sift flour, ¾ cup sugar, 3 tablespoons cocoa, baking powder and salt into a large bowl. Stir in milk, vanilla and oil until well blended. Stir in nuts. Pour batter into prepared pan. Mix the 1¼ cups sugar with ¼ cup cocoa and sprinkle over batter. Pour hot water over surface. Bake for 40 to 45 minutes. Spoon out while warm, sauce side up. Top with whipped cream or ice cream.

Mabel Isabel Distad Whipple
Kit Roberts

Preserves & Pickles

MUSTARD

This is a recipe from my husband's grand-mother, Mrs. Andrew Greiner. Josephine Simmons Greiner (1860-1924) was the daughter of William Simmons (1822-c 1895), who crossed the Oregon Trail in 1845 and Tryphena Ann Havird (1838-1924), who crossed the Oregon Trail in 1853. Mrs. Greiner's many descendants still use and enjoy this recipe.

3 tablespoons dry mustard
3 tablespoons water
2 egg yolks or 1 whole egg, beaten
½ cup vinegar
1 tablespoon sugar
Pinch of salt
2 tablespoons butter
(½ teaspoon turmeric if whole egg
    is used)

Dissolve the mustard with the water in the top of a double boiler. Whisk in egg yolks or whole egg, vinegar, sugar and salt. Cook over simmering water, stirring often, until thick. Whisk in butter. If whole egg is used, add turmeric for color. Store in refrigerator.

Eva Lou Greiner

HATTIE'S RASPBERRY SYRUP

10 pounds raspberries
Sugar
¼ cup vinegar

Crush and strain juice from berries. Measure juice, and for each pint of juice add 1 pound sugar. Place juice, sugar and vinegar into a large pot and boil 10 minutes. Pour into clean, hot pint jars leaving ½-inch headspace. Wipe rims and adjust lids. Process in a boiling water bath for 10 minutes.

Gerald W. Frank

APPLE BUTTER

My grandmother was an Oregon pioneer who settled in the Coquille, Oregon area. She made this often and we ate it with homemade bread.

12 pounds tart cooking apples;
    peeled, cored and quartered
2 cups water
2 cups sugar
1½ cups brown sugar
3 teaspoons cinnamon
1½ teaspoons ground cloves
½ teaspoon allspice

Preheat oven to 375 degrees.
Combine apples and water in a large pot and cook over low heat until tender, about 20 minutes. Puree apples through a food mill or sieve. Add remaining ingredients and stir to mix well. Put mixture into a heavy roasting pan and cook, uncovered, in the oven for about 2½ hours, stirring every 15 minutes with a wooden spoon. The apple butter is ready when it rounds slightly on the spoon and is glossy. Pack into hot, sterilized pint jars leaving ¼-inch headspace. Adjust lids and process in a boiling water bath for 10 minutes. Yield: about 7 pints.

Virginia A. Whipple

BEET PICKLES

This recipe has been in the family cookbooks for at least 100 years.

 2 quarts beets
 2 cups vinegar
 1 cup water
 1 cup sugar
 2 tablespoons mixed pickling spices

Cook beets in enough water to cover, until tender. Dip cooked beets in cold water and slip off skins. If beets are very small, keep whole; if not, cut in half or quarters.

Combine remaining ingredients in a large enamel or stainless steel pot and bring to a boil. Add beets and simmer 15 minutes. Pack beets into hot, clean jars and pour in boiling syrup, leaving ½-inch head space. Seal and process 10 minutes in a boiling water bath. Yield: 5 pints.

Elna Elliott Schmidt

SWEET CRABAPPLE PICKLES

 30 crabapples
 3 cups sugar
 1 cup cider vinegar
 1 cup water
 1 teaspoon whole cloves
 1 cinnamon stick, broken in pieces
 ½ teaspoon whole allspice

Cut off blossom end of crabapples. Prick all over with a fork. Place all ingredients in a large stainless steel, or other non-reactive, pot. Bring to a boil and boil for 5 minutes. Pack crabapples into hot, clean pint jars, distributing the spices evenly. Pour boiling syrup over crabapples, leaving ½-inch headspace. Wipe rims and adjust lids. Process in a boiling water bath for 15 minutes. Yield: about 3 pints.

Daraleen Wade

How To Preserve A Husband

Be careful in your selection; do not choose too young, and take only such varieties as have been raised in a good moral atmosphere. When once decided upon and selected, let that part remain forever settled, and give your entire thought to preparation for domestic use.

Some insist on keeping them in a pickle, while others are constantly getting them in hot water. Even poor varieties may be made sweet, tender and good by garnishing with patience, well sweetened with smiles, and flavored with kisses to taste, then wrap well in the mantle of charity; keep warm with a steady fire of domestic devotion, and serve with peaches and cream. When thus prepared they will keep for years.

Dorothy Winn Crawn

BREAD AND BUTTER PICKLES

 6 quarts cucumbers, sliced
 1½ quarts onions, sliced
 ¾ cup pickling salt
 Crushed ice
 1½ quarts distilled vinegar
 3½ cups sugar
 ½ cup whole mustard seed
 ¼ cup whole celery seed
 ½ cup whole pickling spice
 3 tablespoons turmeric

Layer cucumbers, onions, salt and ice alternately and let stand 4 hours. Rinse and drain. Combine vinegar, sugar, and spices in a large stainless steel pot, or other non-reactive pot. Bring to a boil. Add cucumbers and onions and return to a boil. Ladle into hot, sterilized jars leaving ½-inch headspace. Wipe rims and adjust lids. Process in a boiling water bath for 10 minutes.

Gail E. Orell
Hersey House
Ashland, Oregon

CHRISTMAS RELISH

10 large green tomatoes
9 medium onions
9 medium carrots, peeled
5 green bell peppers
4 red bell peppers
4 ribs celery
½ cup non-iodized salt
1 tablespoon whole celery seed
1 tablespoon whole mustard seed
3 cups cider vinegar
6 cups sugar

Grind tomatoes, onions, carrots, green peppers, red peppers and celery to a fine dice. Place in a large stainless steel, or other non-reactive, bowl, and mix in the salt. Let mixture stand 15 minutes. Drain vegetables, squeezing out salt liquid, and discard the liquid. Place vegetables in a large stainless steel, or other non-reactive, pot and stir in celery seed, mustard seed, vinegar and sugar. Bring mixture to a boil, and boil for 3 minutes. Ladle relish into hot, sterilized jars leaving ¼-inch headspace. Wipe rims and adjust lids. Process in a boiling water bath for 10 minutes.

Mary Peters

DILLY BEANS

4 pounds long green beans,
    washed and trimmed
4 hot peppers, fresh
4 cloves garlic, peeled
4 heads dill, fresh
½ cup canning salt
5 cups water
5 cups vinegar

Pack beans, lengthwise, into hot, sterilized quart jars leaving ¼-inch headspace. To each quart add 1 hot pepper, 1 clove garlic and 1 head dill. Combine salt, water and vinegar in a large sauce pan and bring to a boil. Pour boiling liquid over packed beans, leaving ½-inch headspace. Seal and process 10 minutes in a boiling water bath. Yield: 4 quarts.

Robin Kimmel

Mincemeat

Jeanetta and Henry Oliver came from Missouri by wagon train in 1880. Grandma wrote mincemeat recipes for several of her granddaughters, and each a little different, just as she remembered it.

About 5 pounds meat; elk or
    deer meat, cook with salt and
    chop, do not grind.
10 cents worth suet
2 pats of butter
Large pan apples, bellflower the best,
    chop with tin can
2 pounds raisins
2 pounds currants
2 pounds dates
One dozen oranges
One dozen lemons
2 spoons each of cloves, cinnamon
    and mace
2 cans pineapple
Chop all with tin can.
Add one pint brandy or whiskey
Sweeten to taste

Let stand overnight.
Now this is the whole recipe, divide if you like.
Billie Howard

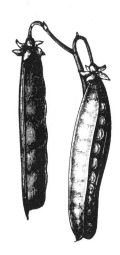

111

GOOSEBERRY CHUTNEY

This chutney enhances the taste of wild game. Elderberries, huckleberries or fresh currants can be substituted for the gooseberries.

4 pounds gooseberries
2 pounds onions, finely chopped
1½ pounds raisins
1 tablespoon fresh ginger, minced
1 teaspoon whole cloves
1 teaspoon whole peppercorns
1 teaspoon whole allspice
1 teaspoon non-iodized salt
1½ cups cider vinegar
2 pounds sugar

Combine gooseberries, onions, raisins, ginger, cloves, peppercorns, allspice, salt and vinegar in a large stainless steel pot, or other non-reactive pot. Bring to a boil then reduce heat to medium and simmer until tender. Add sugar and simmer until thick, about 30 minutes, stirring often. Ladle into hot, sterilized jars leaving ¼-inch headspace. Wipe rims and adjust lids. Process in a boiling water bath for 10 minutes.

Nancy Thornton

EDNA NORTON'S GREEN TOMATO SOY

This is a wonderful relish that is very good on sandwiches.

1 gallon green tomatoes, chopped
    and drained
6 medium onions, finely chopped
2 quarts vinegar
8 cups sugar
2 tablespoons salt
1 teaspoon black pepper
½ teaspoon cloves
½ teaspoon cinnamon

Combine all ingredients in a large stainless steel or other non-reactive pot. Bring to a boil then reduce heat to medium-low and simmer for about 1 hour, stirring often to prevent scorching. Pour into hot, clean pint jars leaving ½-inch headspace. Adjust lids and process in a boiling water bath for 15 minutes.

Bonnie C. Brown

ORANGE MARMALADE

12 thick skinned oranges
3 quarts cold water
8 pounds sugar
Juice of 4 lemons

Slice oranges very thin and discard seeds. Pour over water and let stand in refrigerator 24 hours. Place in a large stainless steel pot, or other non-reactive pot, and bring to a boil. Reduce heat to medium and cook, stirring often, until tender, about 45 minutes. Remove from heat and let cool. Stir in sugar and return to a boil. Reduce heat to medium-low and simmer about 2 hours, or until thickened, stirring often. Just before removing from heat stir in lemon juice. Ladle into hot, sterilized jars leaving 1/4-inch headspace. Wipe rims and adjust lids. Process in boiling water bath for 10 minutes.

Lillian L. Dickinson

JAM AND PRESERVES

Martha Blanch Jeter Goin was two years old when she came across the Oregon Trail in 1865 in a covered wagon. Her parents, Reverend William Jeter and Emiline Thomas Jeter, organized the Baptist Church in Stayton, Oregon.

6 pounds prepared fruit
4½ pounds cane sugar

Mash the fruit with a potato masher. Cook until ready to stick in the bottom of a preserving kettle, stirring all the while. Then add the cane sugar. Boil until it slides to edge of spoon and falls in two or three drops from edge of spoon. In making pear preserves, add 4 or 5 thin slices of lemon including the rind. Seal.

(To seal, ladle hot preserves into hot, sterilized jars leaving 1/4-inch headspace. Wipe rims and adjust lids. Process in a boiling water bath for 10 minutes.)

Mrs. Varion E. (Anna Lee) Goin

MARASCHINO CHERRIES
(Candied Cherries)

My great-great grandfather, Alphonso Boone, had the ferry in Wilsonville, Oregon. He was the grandson of Daniel Boone, the Frontiersman.

5 pounds cherries, pitted
5 pounds sugar
4 cups water
2 ounces red food coloring
2 ounces almond extract

Combine sugar and water in a large pot and bring to a boil. Add cherries and return to a boil. Remove from heat and stir in food coloring and almond extract. Return to heat and bring to a boil again. Remove from heat and let stand 24 hours in the refrigerator. Bring to a rolling boil again, then ladle into hot, sterilized jars leaving 1/2-inch headspace. Wipe rims and adjust lids. Process in a boiling water bath for 5 minutes.

Vera Merwin Schneider Botorf

To Preserve Green Beans For Winter Use

Pick green beans when young and tender. Put a 3-inch layer of them in a small wooden keg. Sprinkle in salt an inch deep, then repeat with beans, alternate to the top. Cover with wooden lid that fits inside of keg. Put a heavy weight, like a big rock on it. Beans will form a brine. When needed, take out amount need and soak overnight or longer, changing water often until salt is out of them. Then cook with bacon.

June Yokum Morris

PICKLED PEARS

6 pounds seckle pears
4 cups white wine vinegar
2½ pounds sugar
½ tablespoon whole cloves
2 sticks cinnamon
Zest of 1 lemon

Peel and stem the pears. Combine vinegar, sugar, cloves, cinnamon and lemon zest in a large stainless steel pot, or other non-reactive pot, and bring to a boil. Add pears and simmer for 5 minutes. Pack pears into hot, sterilized jars and distribute the spices evenly. Pour hot syrup into jars leaving ¼-inch headspace. Wipe rims and adjust lids. Process in a boiling water bath for 10 minutes.

Gerald W. Frank

NEVER FAIL DILL PICKLES

My great-grandparents, James and Mary Savoy Williams, crossed the plains by ox team in 1852.

For each quart:
Cucumbers
1 head fresh dill
3 small cloves garlic
¼ teaspoon pickling spice
¼ teaspoon food-grade alum
1 cup water
1 cup vinegar
2 tablespoons pickling salt

Wash cucumbers and trim off blossom end. Pack cucumbers half full into hot, sterilized quart jars. Add dill, garlic, pickling spice and alum then pack jar full with cucumbers. Place water, vinegar and salt in a stainless steel saucepan and bring to a boil. Pour into jars leaving ½-inch headspace. Wipe rims and adjust lids. Process in boiling water bath for 10 minutes.

Bernice Leffler Fair

114

GRANDMA HOLMAN'S MINCEMEAT

This recipe is from my great-grandmother, Amelia Jane Moss Holman, who came West by covered wagon in 1864 to settle in the LaGrande area. She was nine years old at the time.

3 pounds beef, chopped
1 tablespoon salt
3 pounds raisins
2 pounds currants
2 quarts pie cherries, pitted and
    chopped
9 pounds apples; peeled, cored and
    chopped
1 cup vinegar
4 cups sugar
2 teaspoons cinnamon, or to taste
1 whole nutmeg, ground, or to taste
Cloves if desired

Place beef and salt in a large pot and barely cover with water. Simmer until beef is cooked, occasionally skimming off the scum that rises to the surface. Add remaining ingredients and simmer until slightly thickened, stirring often. Fill hot, sterilized quart jars, leaving 1-inch headspace. Wipe rims and adjust lids. Process in a dial-gauge pressure canner at 11 pounds pressure for 90 minutes if your altitude is 0-2000 feet; or 12 pounds pressure for 90 minutes if your altitude is 2001-4000 feet; or 13 pounds pressure for 90 minutes if your altitude is 4001-6000 feet; or 14 pounds pressure for 90 minutes if your altitude is 6001-8000 feet. For an extra measure of safety you should boil home-canned meats for at least 10 minutes before eating them.

Luella Holman Bennett

PEAR BUTTER

4 cups pear pulp
3 cups sugar
1 orange, juice and zest
½ teaspoon nutmeg

Coarsely chop pulp and put in large preserving kettle with the rest of ingredients. Heat slowly until sugar dissolves, stirring constantly. Bring mixture to a boil and continue cooking until butter thickens. Stir constantly to prevent scorching. Pour cooked pear butter into hot, clean jars leaving ¼-inch headspace. Seal and process 10 minutes in a boiling water bath.

Chris Rossi

PICCALILLI PICKLES

12 onions
8 carrots
2 small heads cabbage
4 red bell peppers
4 green bell peppers
½ cup non-iodized salt
6 cups cider vinegar
6 cups sugar
1 tablespoon whole celery seed
1 tablespoon whole mustard sees

Grind onions, carrots, cabbage, red peppers and green peppers to a fine dice. Place vegetables in a large stainless steel bowl, or other non-reactive bowl and stir in the salt. Let stand 2 hours. Drain the vegetables well, discard the liquid. Place drained vegetables, vinegar, sugar, celery seed and mustard seed in a large stainless steel pot, or other non-reactive pot. Bring to a boil then reduce heat and simmer 15 minutes. Ladle into hot, sterilized jars leaving ½-inch headspace. Wipe rims and adjust lids. Process in boiling water bath for 10 minutes.

Cynthia Berne

PICKLED BEETS

1 gallon small beets
2 cups brown sugar
2 cups water
2 cups vinegar
1 lemon, sliced thin
1 tablespoon cinnamon
1 teaspoon cloves
1 teaspoon allspice

Cook beets in enough water to cover until tender. Dip beets in cold water and slip off skins. If beets are very small, keep whole; if not, cut in half or quarters.

Combine remaining ingredients in large enamel or stainless steel pot and bring to a boil. Add beets and simmer 15 minutes. Pack beets into hot sterilized jars and pour in boiling syrup, leaving ¼-inch head space. Seal and process 10 minutes in a boiling water bath. Yield: 9 pints.

Janice M. Hardy

SPICED CHERRIES

7 pounds cherries, pitted (Royal Anne
        or Black Cherries)
3½ pounds sugar
3 cups vinegar
1 tablespoon whole cloves
1 tablespoon whole allspice
3 cinnamon sticks, broken
        into pieces
1 tablespoon mace

Combine all ingredients in a large stainless steel pot, or other non-reactive pot, and bring to a boil. Reduce heat to medium and cook, stirring often, until thick, about 45 minutes. Ladle into hot, sterilized jars leaving ¼-inch headspace. Wipe rims and adjust lids. Process in boiling water bath for 10 minutes.

Gerald W. Frank

RHUBARB ORANGE MARMALADE

8 pounds rhubarb
1 pound oranges
1 pound sugar
2 cups light corn syrup
1 cup raisins (optional)

Wash rhubarb and cut into 1-inch slices. Wash oranges, cut off ends and discard. Coarsely chop oranges, including the peel. Place all ingredients in a large kettle and simmer until the peel is tender, about 30 minutes. Fill hot, sterilized jars leaving ¼-inch headspace. Seal and process 5 minutes in a boiling water bath.

Chris Rossi

TOMATO CATSUP

2 quarts fresh tomato juice
1 cup vinegar
½ cup sugar
1 tablespoon salt
1 small onion, chopped
1 clove garlic, crushed
1 tablespoon whole cloves
6-inch piece cinnamon stick, broken
        into 1-inch pieces
1 tablespoon whole allspice
¼ teaspoon dried, hot red pepper;
        or to taste

Combine tomato juice, vinegar, sugar and salt in a large stainless steel pot, or other non-reactive pot. Tie up remaining ingredients in a cheesecloth bag and add to pot. Simmer until volume is reduced by one-half or until desired thickness. Remove cheesecloth bag and discard. Ladle catsup into hot, sterilized half-pint jars, leaving ¼-inch headspace. Wipe rims and adjust lids. Process in boiling water bath for 15 minutes.

Vernice Roberts

EMILY'S MINCE MEAT

15 cups apples, chopped
5 cups cooked venison, chopped
3 cups broth in which meat was cooked
2½ cups suet, chopped
3 cups apple cider
½ cup vinegar
1 cup molasses
5 cups sugar
¾ pound citron, finely chopped
2½ cups whole raisins
1½ cups raisins, finely chopped
Dash of salt
Juice of 2 lemons
Juice of 2 oranges
2 tablespoons cinnamon
2 tablespoons allspice
1 tablespoon cloves
1 tablespoon mace
2 whole nutmegs, grated
2 tablespoons lemon extract
1 teaspoon almond extract
1½ cups brandy
Zest of 2 lemons
Zest of 2 oranges

Combine all ingredients, except brandy and zest of lemons and oranges, in a large stainless steel pot, or other non-reactive pot. Simmer for 1½ hours, stirring often. Add brandy and zest of lemons and oranges and bring to a boil. Immediately ladle into hot, sterilized quart jars, leaving 1-inch headspace. Wipe rims and adjust lids. Process in a dial-gauge pressure canner at 11 pounds pressure for 90 minutes if your altitude is 0-2000 feet; or 12 pounds pressure for 90 minutes if your altitude is 2001-4000 feet; or 13 pounds pressure for 90 minutes if your altitude is 4001-6000 feet; or 14 pounds of pressure for 90 minutes if your altitude is 6001-8000 feet. For an extra measure of safety you should boil home-canned meats for at least 10 minutes before eating them.

Gail E. Orell
Hersey House
Ashland, Oregon

Remedies & Receipts

ELIZABETH CAROTHERS RITTER'S ONION SYRUP

My great-grandmother, Elizabeth Carothers, was a girl of thirteen in 1864 when she left her Missouri home and began the walk to Oregon. She was fond of telling the story of the night, long after everyone was asleep, an Indian brave "all naked and painted" stuck his head into her wagon. She feigned sleep until she heard him leave, then dared to peek out and watch him as he crept from wagon to wagon. The next day Elizabeth told her sister of the nocturnal visit, and together they decided the Indian was counting to see how many scalps he could get. They rushed to warn their parents, only to be assured the Indian was only "Lizzie's dream". Perhaps he was only a dream, though Elizabeth often spoke of that shadowy brave in great detail.

Other Trail stories involved illness and death which the Carothers family fought off with Onion Syrup. A batch of this cold remedy was carefully packed among the other medicines necessary for the arduous Oregon Trail. During the spring and summer of 1864, with men, women and children walking all day, often barefoot, through weather ranging from cold driving rain to blistering sun, many sickened and died. If a person couldn't rest at night he didn't get another chance until the following evening. Lack of sleep, hard work and bad weather combined to weaken even the strongest, and small children were even more vulnerable. None of the Carothers children need worry though. They had Onion Syrup.

My father helped his grandmother, Elizabeth Carothers Ritter, make Onion Syrup many times when he was a boy. She learned the recipe from her mother. The syrup is made in the autumn when onions are harvested. Dad told me that Elizabeth would put a five gallon kettle on the back of the wood-burning stove. This she would nearly fill with peeled, whole onions. She then added water to cover and allowed the whole thing to simmer slowly for several days. It was ready when the little bit remaining was the color and consistency of honey. The five gallon kettle produced about two pints of the thick, golden syrup.

Dad swore his grandma's Onion Syrup tasted wonderful, sweet and not like onions at all. If you had a tickle in your throat, a hacking cough or congestion, one tasty spoonful calmed the nastiest of symptoms, made you feel warm inside and out, and induced a deep and restful sleep.

Jeanne Gentry

AN ACCOUNT OF LUCINDA CARNUTT OFFIELD BECKWITH JONES

Life in Clackamas County ca 1851-54

Grandmother was a very capable woman who could do almost anything she set out to do. It wasn't long until she had a good garden, chickens, cows and calves, a pony or two and some sheep. From the sheep she sheared and carded the wool, dyed it and spun it into yarn and knit socks. She also wove it into cloth from which she cut out and sewed garments. Besides eating the meat of the animals, she made crochet needles and hooks and other things from the bone. The first crocheting I ever did was with the splinter of the legbone of a chicken and it worked fine. From the fat of the animals grandmother made soap. She built a hopper in which she placed wood ashes, then poured in the water and drained out the lye to put in the fat to make soap. Grandmother was a mid-wife and doctor for all the neighborhood. She used home remedies, roots, leaves, poultices, etc., and she had good results. There were no trained doctors other than grandma in those days. The family made out well, everyone in the neighborhood helped everyone else.

Dave R. Grafe

Mrs. Richard Lee (Mary Adaline) Cannon

"In 1854 I was three months old, when, with my parents, we headed for Oregon by ox team and prairie schooner. I have lived on a farm all my life. I have never bought butter but once since I was married. We put up our own bacon and hams. We raise our own chickens and turkeys as well as having all the eggs, butter, fruit, vegetables, grapes, berries, cherries and walnuts we can use. Occasionally we kill an Angora kid or yearling calf, but for the most part we eat chicken, eggs, bacon or ham. I suppose there are many people who live daintier than we do and have more money, but I doubt if there are many people who have better appetites and more satisfying food than we do."

Justine L. Jones
The Oregon Journal November 10, 1930

SNOW ICE CREAM

Collect a very large bowl of freshly fallen, clean snow. Sugar as you would a huge bowl of oatmeal. Add a little cream and some kind of flavoring, such as: vanilla, peanut butter, maple syrup, molasses, berries or berry syrup.

Use your imagination, settle back and enjoy!

Inez Miller

BLACKBERRY WINE

Take ripe berries and press out the juice through a coarse cloth. To every quart juice add one quart water, in which has been dissolved two pounds of white sugar. Put in glass bottles or jugs and cover the mouth with any open meshed cloth to admit air and keep out insects. Set in the cellar for six months, more or less. Then pour off carefully from the sediments. Put in clean bottles and cork up for use.

Justine Jones

RASPBERRY SHRUB

My great-great-grandmother, Polly Bowen, came to Oregon in a covered wagon with her eight siblings. Her parents died along the way. The rest arrived here in 1853.

In a large glass or ceramic bowl, stir together 4 quarts crushed red raspberries and 1 quart vinegar. Cover and let stand for 4 days. Strain and discard solids. To each pint of juice add 1 pound of sugar. Put in a large stainless steel or other non-reactive pot, and boil for 20 minutes. Pour into sterile bottles and seal. Keep in a dry, cool place.

Betsy Noah

SUNDAY SUPPER

Prepare cornmeal with water in saucepan according to directions for cornmeal mush. When cooked, drop into a tall glass of milk, a spoonful at a time. Salt, and eat with a spoon.

Emily Houston Savage
Gail E. Orell
Hersey House
Ashland, Oregon

BEDTIME SNACK

Butter a piece of bread. Slice mild onions and place on top for open-face onion sandwich. A red onion or other mild onion is preferred.

Gail E. Orell
Hersey House
Ashland, Oregon

GRAVEYARD STEW

Milk Toast for upset tummies.

1 slice bread, toasted and buttered
¾ cup milk, heated but not boiled
Sugar to taste

Place toast in a bowl, sprinkle with sugar and pour warmed milk over toast.

Gail E. Orell
Hersey House
Ashland, Oregon

SCRAPED APPLE

For sick children.

Cut apple in half. Taking a dull table knife, scrape the apple-meat a bite at a time. Feed it to the ill person (on the knife) until only the outer peel remains. Delicious, and makes one feel very loved and special.

Gail E. Orell
Hersey House
Ashland, Oregon

LAKE COUNTY SLOUGH JUICE

James Houston is a descendant of Robert Houston who came across the Oregon Trail in 1847 to settle in the Albany, Oregon area. Robert Houston was called "Squire Houston" and was the first Justice of the Peace in Albany. He also helped found the first school district and served on the school board.

1 fifth Vodka
2 quarts sparkling water
1 16-ounce can frozen lemonade

Put in gallon jug and fill with ice cubes. Don't drink too much.

James F. Houston
Gail E. Orell
Hersey House
Ashland, Oregon

TAFFY ON THE SNOW

2 cups sugar
½ cup water
1 teaspoon vanilla

Cook the sugar and water together until the hard-crack stage, 290 degrees. Stir in the vanilla. Take outside and spoon onto clean, fresh snow. Everyone follows the cook with a spoon to scoop up the candy.

Gail E. Orell
Hersey House
Ashland, Oregon

HEADACHE CURE

Slice one slice from a fresh cucumber. Apply to the forehead, it will adhere. The cucumber is both soothing and curing for a mild headache.

Gail E. Orell
Hersey House
Ashland, Oregon

LUXURIOUS BATH WATER

Place ½ cup of uncooked oatmeal in a square of cheesecloth or other porous cloth. Secure with a bow. Add to the bath water to soften the water and the skin.

Gail E. Orell
Hersey House
Ashland, Oregon

SCARLET FEVER REMEDY

Bathe the child daily in olive oil. It keeps the skin soft, lessens the fever and nourishes the patient. Use little medicine.

Eva Emery Dye
Dolly Hutchinson

RECEIPTS

My husband's grandparents, John M. and Mary Louisa Black, came across the plains in a wagon train in 1865. Mary Louisa kept a diary of their journey in a small leather-bound notebook. There are many notes in the little book: farm records, family records, dates of her babies' births, directions for weaving cloth, knitting socks, and recipes and remedies. These are some of her receipts in her own words and spelling.

Cake.. 2 cups sugar.. ½ cup butter.. ¼ cup sourdough.. ½ teaspoon soda.. nutmeg.

Recept for Ginger Cake: 1 pt molasses.. 4 eggs.. 1 cup sugar.. 1 tablespoon ginger.. ½ pt butter.. ½ pt sour cream.. tablespoon soda.. should be thick as pound cake.

Recept for Ginger Snaps.. To one quart of molasses, add one pint of butter, one tablespoon ginger, one teaspoonful of soda, flour to make a stiff dough.. role thin and bake in a quick oven.

A doctor friend of the family gave Mary Louisa a supply of drugs and directions for their use. Here is an example:
Mountain Fever. This is the easiest thing treated in the world. You first give a very active purgative, nearly a double dose af McLean's Pills or Blue Moss and Calomel combined, then 40 drops of Laudanum. Sponge the body often with tepid water. Repeat the Laudanum from 25 to 40 drops so as to keep the patient under the influence of it 48 hours. Then if there be any fever left, repeat the purgative, followed by more Laudanum.

Marguerite and John M. Black II

CANDLES

This is from a diary my great-grandfather, Philamon Morris, kept while coming to Oregon in 1853.

A receipt for to make candles out of lard. Take 8 lbs of lard and melt it. Blood warm one ounce of akuque fortis (aqua fortis - nitric acid), pore in, heat it till the fram dose rise. Skim it and mold your candles. And they will bee equal to the spirm candles.

Mildred Hansen

FOR A BURN

This is quoted from the journal of my great-great-grandmother Maria Morfitt Locey

2 egg whites
1 tablespoon salt

Beat the egg whites with the salt well. Saturate cotton and apply to the burn.

Carole Parkinson

COUGH SYRUP

1 whole lemon
2 tablespoons glycerin
Honey

Boil the lemon in water slowly for 10 minutes. Cut in half and extract the juice with a lemon reamer. Pour in a drinking glass and add the glycerin. Stir well then fill the glass with honey.

Janice M. Hardy

DIGESTIVE AID

2 teaspoons honey
2 teaspoons cider vinegar

Stir together in a 12 ounce glass. Fill with water and drink.

Janice M. Hardy

CURE FOR A HEADACHE

The following remedy is from the diary of my great-great-grandfather, Philemon Morris. He traveled with his wife and children along the Oregon Trail and Barlow Road in 1852. They settled on a land donation claim in the Sublimity, Oregon area. The spelling is as it was originally written.

A certen cure for a sur pain in the head. Shave a plais on the top of your head. And take and cut around peas of thin leather as big as a dollar. Spread some beefs gall on the leather and stick it on your head and it will affect a cure. Let it stic till it comes off. Perhaps it will bee 2 or 3 weeks.

Connie L. Rodgers

TO REMOVE WARTS

Get a long piece of black sewing thread. Wad it up. Rub over wart. Hide it under a rock. When it rots the wart will be gone. Don't tell anyone you did it or it won't work.

J. Mitchell Russell

RECEIPT FOR COUGH SYRUP

This recipe was given to me by my mother, Leota Mitchell, in 1944. It has been in the family since my great-grandmother's time.

1 cup weak vinegar, weak enough so
it doesn't strangle anyone
2 tablespoons brown sugar
1 teaspoon honey, if you have it
Good butter the size of a marble

Mix everything up and heat to dissolve. Give it as often as you want. This beats all the modern cough medicine there is.

J. Mitchell Russell

Northwest Chefs

FRESH RASPBERRY TEA BREAD

Many of the wagon trains that rolled over the Oregon Trail brought families from the Midwest and South who settled outside Portland. The county names in Oregon, such as Polk, Jefferson, Jackson, and Lincoln, reflect their influence. Portland itself was settled by New Englanders who arrived on boats. (The name "Portland" came from the flip of a coin: Was the new city to be named Portland, after Portland, Maine, or Boston, after Boston, Massachusetts?) English Yankees loved their afternoon tea, and in the nineteenth century the serving of afternoon tea was common in Portland. Today, Portland's Heathman Hotel has revived the tradition. The following recipe for raspberry tea bread produces a moist bread with a lovely sweet cardamom aftertaste. It could easily be served as a dessert with a Pacific Northwest late-harvest Riesling.

> ¾ cup fresh raspberries
> ⅓ cup raspberry liqueur
> 1 cup plus 1 tablespoon sugar
> 8 tablespoons corn oil margarine or
>   butter (½ cup)
> 1 egg
> 1½ cups all-purpose flour
> 1 teaspoon ground cardamom
> 2 teaspoons baking soda
> ⅓ cup buttermilk

Preheat the oven to 350 degrees and grease an 8 x 3¾ x 2½-inch loaf pan. Macerate the raspberries in the raspberry liqueur for 30 minutes. Cream 1 cup sugar with the butter. Add the egg and beat well. Stir in the flour, cardamom, baking soda, and buttermilk. Drain the raspberries, reserving the liqueur, and carefully fold them into the batter. Pour the batter into the prepared pan and drizzle with the liqueur. Sprinkle with the remaining tablespoon of sugar and bake for 45 minutes.

Food Processor Method:

Preheat the oven to 350 degrees and grease a loaf pan. Macerate the raspberries in the raspberry liqueur for 30 minutes. Put 1 cup of sugar and the butter in the work bowl and pulse 8 to 10 times.

Add the egg and process for 30 seconds. In a small bowl stir the flour, cardamom and baking soda together. Sprinkle the dry ingredients over the creamed sugar and process for 30 seconds. With the machine still running, gradually pour in the buttermilk. Pour the batter into the prepared pan. Drain the berries, reserving the liqueur, and carefully fold in the berries. Drizzle the liqueur over the batter and sprinkle with the reserved tablespoon of sugar. Bake for 45 minutes.

Janie Hibler, Author
Dungeness Crabs and Blackberry Cobblers
Portland, Oregon

OREGON PRUNE JAM

Prune's sweet, almost earthy flavor make delectable jam. This is delicious on corn muffins, combined with apples for a pie, or folded into whipped cream. Toss in a few toasted, halved hazelnuts and use several tablespoons in roast goose stuffing. Reduce the amount of sugar if your prefer.

> 2½ pounds pitted prunes
> 2½ to 3 cups sugar
> ½ teaspoon allspice
> ½ teaspoon cloves
> ½ teaspoon cinnamon
> ¼ teaspoon nutmeg
> 1 cup cider vinegar

In a bowl, mix the pitted prunes, sugar, and spices together. Pour the vinegar into a stainless steel saucepan, add the prune mixture, and cook slowly over low heat, stirring frequently to prevent sticking, until the jam thickens and coats the back of a spoon. Pour into prepared jars and cover tightly. Yield: 4 cups.

Emily Crumpacker, Author
Seasonal Gifts from the Kitchen
Portland, Oregon

FIG ALMOND RELISH

During autumn, the tree outside our kitchen window is laden with figs, and I always make this relish. The unusual combination of the almond texture with the sweet fig flavor will bring a cold meat dish or a mild curry to life.

2½ pounds fresh figs, stems discarded and cut into ¼-inch slices
2 cups sugar
¼ cup orange juice
Zest from one orange
1 cinnamon stick, broken into small pieces
2 whole cloves
2 whole allspice
⅓ cup cider vinegar
½ cup almonds, coarsely chopped and toasted

In a 4-quart stainless-steel pot, combine the figs, sugar, orange juice, and zest. Allow to stand at room temperature for 2 to 3 hours. Place the spices in cheesecloth and tie tightly. Bring the fruit mixture to a boil. Reduce heat, add spice bag and vinegar. Simmer gently, stirring carefully, for 30 minutes. Add almonds and remove from heat. Remove spices and cool; pour into prepared jars and seal. Yield: 2½ cups.

Emily Crumpacker, Author
Seasonal Gifts from the Kitchen
Portland, Oregon

WALNUT CRANBERRY BREAD

This is my husband's favorite quick bread; the piquant combination of flavors is lovely as morning toast, an afternoon accompaniment to tea, and as a holiday bread at Christmas. Frozen cranberries work very nicely and, if the bread is well wrapped, it can be frozen for several months.

2 tablespoons butter
1 cup sugar
1 egg, lightly beaten
2 oranges, zested
¾ cup orange juice
2 cups flour
½ teaspoon salt
½ teaspoon baking soda
1½ teaspoons baking powder
1 cup whole cranberries
¾ cup chopped walnuts

Cream the butter and sugar together, add the beaten egg, then the orange juice and zest. Sift the remaining dry ingredients together. Dust the cranberries and nuts with 1 extra tablespoon flour. Blend the sugar-orange mixture with the sifted dry ingredients. Stir in nuts and cranberries. Pour batter into a medium loaf pan that has been greased and floured; bake at 325 degrees for 1 to 1¼ hours.

Emily Crumpacker, Author
Seasonal Gifts from the Kitchen
Portland, Oregon

STURGEON STARK STREET

½ cup Beurre Blanc Sauce (page 135)
6 medallions of sturgeon,
        2 to 3 ounces each
Flour to dust
Oil for frying
2 tablespoons chopped fresh basil
1 tablespoon Dijon mustard
1 teaspoon cracked black peppercorns

Prepare the Buerre Blanc and reserve. Dust sturgeon medallions with flour. Cook the sturgeon in a small amount of oil over high heat to sear and brown. This should require no more than 1 to 2 minutes per side. Reduce heat to low, pour off the excess oil and add the Buerre Blanc, basil, mustard and pepper. Swirl to blend the sauce and coat the medallions.

Approximate preparation time: 20 minutes.
Yield: 2 servings.

Whitney Peterson, Executive Chef
Jake's Famous Crawfish
Portland, Oregon

CRAB LEG SAUTÉ

¼ cup Bearnaise Sauce (page 135)
3 tablespoons butter
10 to 12 mushrooms, sliced
        (about 1¼ cups)
2 teaspoons minced garlic
4 cooked artichoke hearts, cut in half
4 green onions, chopped
        (about 4 tablespoons)
¼ cup sherry
Salt and pepper to taste
8 ounces dungeness crab leg meat

Prepare Bearnaise Sauce and reserve. Melt 2 tablespoons of the butter in a sauté pan over medium to high heat and sauté mushrooms for 1 minute. Add garlic, artichoke hearts and green onions. Continue sautéing for another minute. Add sherry, salt and pepper and simmer another 3 minutes. Divide the mixture into 2 serving casseroles or boats. Return the sauté pan to the heat and add remaining butter and the crab legs. Heat for 2 minutes. Spoon the crab leg meat over the vegetables and top each boat with 1 to 2 tablespoons of Bearnaise.

Approximate preparation time: 10 minutes for the Bearnaise Sauce, 15 minutes for the sauté.
Yield: 2 servings.

Whitney Petersen, Executive Chef
Jake's Famous Crawfish
Portland, Oregon

SOLE PARMESAN

½ cup flour
1 egg, beaten with 1 tablespoon milk
6 to 8 ounces fresh shredded Parmesan
    (canned, grated cheese
    will *not* work)
1 cup flaked, dried bread crumbs
12 to 16 ounces boneless filet of sole
    (preferably petrale)
3 tablespoons oil for frying
2 tablespoons butter
2 tablespoons lemon juice
6 lemon segments, chopped
2 teaspoons capers
1 teaspoon chopped shallots
1 tablespoon chopped parsley

Place the flour, egg and shredded parmesan mixed with the bread crumbs in 3 separate baking dishes. (As noted, the parmesan must be freshly shredded, into thin pieces similar to ½-inch long toothpicks, *not* grated into granules or a powder.) Dip the filets in flour first, shaking off excess, then into egg and finally in the cheese, taking great care to coat the fish evenly and completely. Heat the oil in a large non-stick sauté pan or on a range-top griddle over high heat. Place fish in pan and allow to brown, about 2 minutes. Turn fish, taking care not to disturb the crisply browned cheese. (If the coating flakes off the fish in spots, retrieve the specks of cheese and scatter them back on top of the fish.) After turning the fish will take only 1 more minute. Remove to dinner plates. Wipe oil from pan and return it to the stove or, if using the griddle, heat a sauté pan. Add remaining ingredients and cook over medium heat until the butter is slightly browned. Pour over fish.

Approximate preparation time: 20 minutes.

NOTE: If the pan is not hot enough or the wrong cheese is used, the coating will gum up and ruin the fish.

Whitney Petersen, Executive Chef
Jake's Famous Crawfish
Portland, Oregon

TORTELLONI WITH CRAB AND GORGONZOLA

½ pound dry or 1 pound fresh tortelloni,
    cheese filled, precooked,
    rinsed and drained
6 ounces dungeness crab meat
6 ounces gorgonzola cheese
2 tablespoons butter
2 teaspoons minced shallots
¼ cup dry white wine
½ cup cream
Salt and pepper to taste
1 tablespoon chopped parsley

Pick over the crab meat to remove any lingering shell fragments. Set aside ⅓ of the crab for a garnish. Crumble the cheese. Sauté the shallots in butter over low heat until softened. Add wine and cream and heat to a boil. Add crumbled cheese and ⅔ of the crab. Reduce the sauce over high heat for 1 minute. Add the tortelloni and continue cooking over high heat for another 2 minutes. Season with salt and pepper and remove to dinner plates. Garnish the tortelloni with reserved crab and sprinkle with chopped parsley.

Approximate preparation time: 20 minutes.
Serves 2.

Whitney Petersen, Executive Chef
Jake's Famous Crawfish
Portland, Oregon

SWORDFISH CASINO

½ cup Beurre Blanc Sauce (page 135)
2 swordfish steaks, 1-inch thick,
　　5 to 6 ounces each
3 ounces dungeness crab meat
2 tablespoons roasted red peppers,
　　julienne cut
1 teaspoon lemon juice
2 tablespoons fresh basil leaves,
　　finely shredded
Pinch salt
Pinch pepper

Preheat oven to 400 degrees. Prepare the Beurre Blanc. Cut a slit in the swordfish steaks to form a pocket, as you might for stuffed pork chops. Combine crab, roasted peppers, lemon, basil and salt and pepper to make the stuffing. Divide between the pockets of the 2 steaks. If you have a range-top system like a Jenn-Aire, you can "mark" the swordfish with the grill's crosshatching.

Marked or not, bake in the oven for 10 minutes. Remove to dinner plates and coat each steak with 2 tablespoons beurre blanc.
　Approximate preparation time: 20 minutes.
　Yield: 2 servings.

Whitney Peterson,
Executive Chef
Jake's Famous Crawfish
Portland, Oregon

SWORDFISH PEPPERSTEAK

2 swordfish steaks, 6 to 8 ounces each
2 to 3 tablespoons green peppercorns,
　　drained
3 tablespoons butter
½ cup sliced mushrooms
½ cup tomato, peeled, seeded and diced
3 tablespoons brandy
4 tablespoons cream
Pinch fresh rosemary

Preheat oven to 400 degrees. Press the peppercorns into only 1 side of each swordfish steak. Melt 2 tablespoons butter in a sauté pan over medium-high heat. Place swordfish, pepper-side down, in the pan for 2 minutes to sear. (This will also adhere the peppercorns to the fish.) If a few peppercorns fall off, that's okay. Leave them in the pan for the sauce.

Remove the swordfish to a baking dish, pepper-side up, and finish in the oven for 5 to 6 minutes. Meanwhile, add 1 tablespoon butter to the sauté pan and sauté mushrooms for 1 minute. Add diced tomato and cook for 30 seconds on medium heat. Add brandy and cook for another 30 seconds. Then add cream and rosemary and simmer for 2 to 3 minutes. Remove swordfish to dinner plates, pour the sauce over them and serve.
　Approximate preparation time: 15 minutes.
　Yield: 2 servings.

Whitney Petersen,
Executive Chef
Jake's Famous Crawfish
Portland, Oregon

COD CAKES WITH FRESH APPLESAUCE

1 pound true cod or ling cod,
    poached and cooled
1 stalk celery, finely diced
½ small onion, finely diced
    (about ¼ cup)
½ teaspoon thyme
¼ teaspoon minced garlic
Pinch salt
Pinch pepper
1 egg
2 tablespoons mayonnaise
1 cup bread crumbs
3 tablespoons oil for frying

Applesauce:
2 tablespoons butter
2 tart green apples, peeled and diced
    (about 3 cups)
1 tablespoon lemon juice
½ cup water
3 tablespoons sugar
½ teaspoon cinnamon

Flake the cod and combine with the next 8 ingredients. Blend well and shape into 4 cakes, 3½-inches wide by 1-inch thick. Pat and press bread crumbs into the cakes. While you prepare the applesauce, chill the cakes in the refrigerator. Melt butter in a sauté pan and add apples, lemon juice, water, sugar and cinnamon. Cook over high heat until the liquids evaporate and the apples soften. Set aside. Heat oil in another sauté pan over medium heat and fry the cod cakes for 4 minutes per side until they are crisp, brown and heated through. Serve with the applesauce on the side.

Approximate preparation time: 40 minutes.
Yield: 4 cakes, 3½-inches x 1-inch.

Whitney Petersen, Executive Chef
Jake's Famous Crawfish
Portland, Oregon

DUNGENESS CRAB CAKES

1½ pounds crab meat, picked over
    for shells
1 cup plain bread crumbs
2 celery stalks, finely minced
1 small onion, finely minced
1 small green pepper, finely minced
1 teaspoon dry mustard
½ teaspoon Tabasco
1 large egg
¼ cup mayonnaise
1 tablespoon lemon juice
½ teaspoon Worcestershire sauce
Additional bread crumbs for coating
    the crab cakes
½ cup oil for frying (or more)
1 cup Tartar Sauce or
    Jalapeno Hollandaise (page 136)

Preheat oven to 200 degrees. Combine all the ingredients except the additional bread crumbs for coating, the oil and the tartar sauce. Form the mixture into 8 3-inches to 3½-inches by 1-inch thick crab cakes or 30 to 40 hors d'oeuvres. Coat cakes on both sides with the additional bread crumbs, patting the crumbs lightly into the cakes. If you are making large cakes, put about ¼ cup oil into a 10-inch to 12-inch sauté pan and cook over medium heat. Cook 4 cakes at a time, 4 minute per side. They should be nicely browned on both sides and heated through. Keep the 4 cooked cakes warm in the oven while you prepare the remaining 4. Use fresh oil for the second batch.

Yield: 8 cakes, 3½-inches in diameter or 30 to 40 mini cakes for hor d'oeuvres.

Whitney Petersen, Executive Chef
Jake's Famous Crawfish
Portland, Oregon

BEURRE BLANC SAUCE

6 ounces white wine
3 ounces white wine vinegar
3 whole peppercorns
1 shallot, cut into quarters
1 cup heavy cream
6 ounces cold, unsalted butter, cut into
    pieces
3 ounces cold, butter, cut into pieces

Combine wine, vinegar, peppercorns and shallot in a noncorrosive saucepan (stainless steel, teflon, calphalon).

Reduce over medium heat until the mixture is just 1 to 2 tablespoons and has the consistency of syrup.

Add cream and reduce again until mixture is 3 to 4 tablespoons and very syrupy. Remove from heat.

Add butters, about 2 ounces at a time, stirring constantly and allowing each addition to melt in before adding more. (If mixture cools too much, butter will not melt completely and you will have to reheat slightly.)

Strain and hold warm on a stove-top trivet or in a double-boiler over very low heat until you are ready to use it.

NOTE: This sauce may be flavored with orange, lemon, spices, herbs, berry or fruit concentrates. These may be added at the end or during the reduction of the cream.

Makes about 1 cup.

Whitney Petersen, Executive Chef
Jake's Famous Crawfish
Portland, Oregon

JAKE'S HOLLANDAISE SAUCE

½ pound unsalted butter, melted and
    warm, but not hot
3 egg yolks
1 tablespoon water
1 tablespoon lemon juice
Pinch salt

Melt butter and reserve. Combine the egg yolks and water in the top of a double boiler over hot, but not boiling water, and stir briskly with a wire whisk until the mixture is light and fluffy and the consistency of light mayonnaise.

Remove the top of the double boiler from the heat and slowly add the butter in a thin stream, while continuing to whip the mixture.

Season the mixture with the lemon juice and salt to taste.

Makes about 1½ cup.

Whitney Petersen, Executive Chef
Jake's Famous Crawfish
Portland, Oregon

BEARNAISE SAUCE

¼ cup tarragon vinegar
3 sprigs fresh tarragon
    (or 1 teaspoon dried)
3 sprigs fresh chervil
    (or 1 teaspoon dried)
2 shallots, finely chopped

Combine the vinegar, herbs and shallots over medium heat and reduce to approximately 1 tablespoon of thick paste. Allow to cool slightly. Add paste to Jake's Hollandaise Sauce (above) in place of lemon juice.

Makes about 1½ cup.

Whitney Petersen
Jake's Famous Crawfish
Portland, Oregon

JALAPENO HOLLANDAISE

Proceed as for Hollandaise (page 135), but add one very finely minced jalapeno pepper to the egg and water mixture cooking in the double boiler. Makes about 1½ cups.

Whitney Petersen, Executive Chef
Jake's Famous Crawfish
Portland, Oregon

TARTAR SAUCE

⅓ cup finely minced celery
⅓ cup finely minced onion
2 cups mayonnaise, homemade or
    commercial
2 tablespoons lemon juice
1 teaspoon Worcestershire sauce
Pinch salt
Pinch dry mustard
Pinch pepper
2 tablespoons dill pickle relish

Combine all ingredients and mix well. Makes approximately 3 cups.

Whitney Petersen, Executive Chef
Jake's Famous Crawfish
Portland, Oregon

SHAKER'S CAFE CUSTARD PIE

⅓ cup sugar
2 teaspoons flour
½ teaspoon salt
3 whole large eggs
2 large egg yolks
¼ teaspoon nutmeg (preferably
    freshly grated)
3 cups scalded half & half
1 tablespoon real vanilla
1 unbaked 9-inch pie shell

Mix first six ingredients together until smooth. Add 1 cup of the hot half & half to the egg mixture incorporating completely, then add the remaining 2 cups of half & half and the vanilla. Fill the unbaked shell with custard and bake in middle of 350 degree oven 40 to 50 minutes. Sprinkle with nutmeg.

Jeani Subotnick
Shaker's Cafe
Portland, Oregon

SHAKER'S CAFE GIANT GINGERBREAD MUFFINS

¾ cup sugar
3¾ cups all purpose flour
2¼ teaspoons baking soda
1½ teaspoons cinnamon
1½ teaspoons ginger
¾ teaspoon salt
½ teaspoon nutmeg
2 whole eggs
1½ cups unsulphured molasses
1½ cups buttermilk
¾ cup melted unsalted butter

Preheat oven to 350 degrees. Grease 12 giant muffin tins.

Combine first seven ingredients in medium size bowl. In a separate bowl, mix eggs, molasses, buttermilk and melted butter. Make a well in the center of the dry ingredients, add the wet ingredients to the dry until *just* blended (do not overmix). Spoon into tins, bake 25 to 30 minutes until tested with a toothpick comes out clean. Serve warm with whipped cream.

Jeani Subotnick
Shaker's Cafe
Portland, Oregon

SHAKER'S CAFE OLD TIME RHUBARB CRUNCH

2 cups all purpose flour
2 cups regular rolled oats
2 cups Shakers Cafe Granola*
¼ teaspoon salt
1 cup (2 cubes) unsalted butter
6 cups rhubarb cut into 1-inch squares
1 teaspoon cinnamon
1¼ cups sugar
4 tablespoons cornstarch
½ cup water
1 teaspoon real vanilla

Grease and flour an 11x13½ inch x 1½inch pan.

Mix together the first four dry ingredients in medium size bowl. With fingers rub the butter into the dry ingredients until coarse crumbs form. Reserve 2 cups of crumbs. Pour remaining crumbs into prepared pan. Press firmly into pan until even.

In medium sized heavy bottomed saucepan, cover the rhubarb with cinnamon, sugar, cornstarch and water. Cook over medium heat until thickened and clear. Pour over prepared crust. Top with reserved crumbs. Bake in moderate 350 degree oven 1 hour until thick and bubbly.

*Any good quality oat based granola can be substituted.

Jeani Subotnick
Shaker's Cafe
Portland, Oregon

SPRING RUN CHINOOK TARTARE

1 pound very fresh Chinook salmon fillet
1½ teaspoons grated fresh horseradish
1 tablespoon capers
Juice of 1 lemon
¼ cup minced onion
2 tablespoons chopped parsley
1 anchovy, minced
½ teaspoon prepared stone-ground
    mustard
2 teaspoons olive oil
Dash of Tabasco sauce (or other
    red pepper sauce)
Salt and pepper to taste

Remove any skin or bones from salmon fillet. Cut into 1-inch cubes. Place the salmon in a food processor with all the other ingredients and process in short bursts until well combined. Do not pureé the mixture. Alternatively, the salmon cubes may be minced with a knife to a uniform coarse texture.

Serve with toast points or crackers. Add a well-chilled champagne to complement this elegant appetizer.

Yield: 6-8 servings.

Approximate preparation time: 20 minutes.

Leif Eric Benson, Chef
Timberline Lodge

WALLA WALLA SWEET ONION & HAM TART

The Timberline Lodge at the foot of Mt. Hood in Oregon, is arguably one of the most beautiful lodges in North America. Built during the Works Progress Administration, the craftsmanship, detailing and sheer size have earned the building status of a National Historic Landmark.

3 medium Walla Walla sweet onions,
    thinly sliced
2 tablespoons butter
1 tablespoon caraway seed
8 ounces ham, diced
2 cups sliced mushrooms
¼ cup flour
4 eggs
½ cup cream
¼ cup apricot preserves
1 10-inch tart pastry, unbaked

Cook the onions in the butter for 20 minutes or until golden brown. Add the caraway seed, ham, and mushrooms. Sauté for 10 minutes, add flour and mix well. Remove from heat.

Beat the eggs and mix in the cream. Add to the onion mixture. Pour into tart shell and bake at 350 degrees for 30-45 minutes. (If desired, for the last 10-15 minutes, top with additional thinly sliced onion circles.) Glaze by brushing heated apricot preserves over the top. Return to oven for another 10-15 minutes. Cool before cutting into wedges.

Yield: 6-8 servings.

Leif Eric Benson, Chef
Timberline Lodge

JUANITA'S SPOONBREAD

Spoonbread is a popular dish in the southern United States and conceivably could have travelled with the pioneers of the Oregon Trail. This is my grandmother Juanita Thomas' recipe and was served often in our family. I like to serve it with grilled quail (page 139) giving it an Italian feel, since in Italy roasted or grilled birds are often served with polenta, a cornmeal mush. And come to think of it, the pioneers could have hunted for quail or grouse, and maybe even seasoned it with sagebrush and juniper berries, and wrapped it in bacon from their larder.

2 cups water
1 cup cornmeal
2 tablespoons sugar
1 teaspoon salt
1 cup milk
2 eggs, lightly beaten
1 teaspoon baking powder
4 tablespoons shortening

Boil water. In a medium sized bowl combine cornmeal, sugar and salt. Pour over the boiling water and stir until there are no lumps. Let cool, then add milk and beat well. Add eggs and beat well. Add baking powder. Melt shortening in a cast iron frying pan. Pour mixture into pan while fat is sizzling hot. Bake in 350 degree oven about 25 minutes.

Catherine Whims
Genoa Restaurant
Portland, Oregon

GUALGLIE ALLO SPIEDO
(Grilled Quail with Bacon, Sage and Juniper)

8 whole quail
¼ cup olive oil
1 tablespoon chopped fresh sage or
     ½ tablespoons dried sage
8 juniper berries, crushed
1 teaspoon black peppercorns,
     crushed in a mortar and pestle
¼ teaspoons salt
8 thin slices bacon

Combine the oil, sage, juniper, salt and pepper. Dry each quail with a towel and rub with the marinade inside and out. Let sit 2 hours or overnight in refrigerator.

Prepare charcoal grill or heat broiler. Wrap bacon around the bodies of the quail. Skewer 2 quail through the bacon onto metal skewers. Cook until skin is nicely brown and meat is done. Serve with Juanita's spoonbread (page 138).

Catherine Whims
Genoa Restaurant
Portland, Oregon

SAVORY COEUR À LA CRÈME

1½ pounds cream cheese, softened
½ cup crème fraiche or sour cream
½ cup sun dried tomatoes packed
     in olive oil, minced
1 tablespoon white wine vinegar
3 cloves garlic, minced
1 teaspoon dill
1 teaspoon tarragon
½ teaspoon salt
½ teaspoon white pepper
Water crackers as an accompaniment
Grapes as an accompaniment

In a large bowl, combine all ingredients and stir to blend well. Line a 2-quart heart shaped mold with plastic wrap. Press mixture into mold and chill at least 12 hours. To serve, unmold onto a serving platter and surround with water crackers and grapes.

Whipple & Wied Catering, Inc.
Lake Oswego, Oregon

ECLAIRS

I learned to make these from Christian Guillut and Bruno Neveu at the Ecole de Gastronomie Française Ritz-Escoffier in Paris.

Pâte à Choux
    ½ cup water
    ½ cup milk
    ½ cup butter, unsalted
    ¼ teaspoon salt
    1 cup flour, sifted
    1 cup eggs, beaten

Crème Pâtissière
    2 cups milk
    ⅔ cup sugar
    1 vanilla bean, split
    6 egg yolks
    2½ tablespoons flour
    2½ tablespoons cornstarch
    4 tablespoons butter

Glaçage Miroir au Chocolat
    1 cup cream
    7 ounces semi-sweet chocolate, chopped
    6 tablespoons clarified butter

Preheat oven to 400 degrees. Lightly grease baking sheets.

For the Pâte à Choux: Bring the water, milk, butter and salt to a boil. Remove from heat and add the flour all at once, stirring with a wooden spoon. Mixture will form a mass and pull away from the sides of the pan. Add beaten eggs a little at a time, beating well with a wooden spoon after each addition. The batter is the right consistency when you dip your finger into the warm batter then pull it out and hold it upright; if the batter stands up in a point, it is too stiff; if it drops over and forms a hook, it is just right. Fill pastry bag with the batter and pipe onto prepared baking sheets. Brush tops with beaten egg mixed with a little water. Bake for about 20 to 30 minutes or until golden brown.

For the Crème Pâtissière: In a sauce pan, bring the milk, 5 tablespoons of the sugar and vanilla bean to a boil. In a bowl, whisk together the egg yolks and remaining sugar until foamy. Sift the flour and cornstarch into the egg yolks and blend. Remove vanilla bean. Ladle some of the hot milk into the egg mixture and whisk to dilute, then pour all into the sauce pan. Reduce heat and cook, whisking vigorously, until thick. Remove from heat and whisk in butter. Cover with plastic wrap and cool completely.

For the Glaçage Miroir au Chocolat: In a sauce pan, bring the cream to a boil. Pour over chocolate and whisk until smooth. Whisk in clarified butter. Keep warm in a double boiler.

Pierce a small hole in the bottom of the Choux pastries. Fill a pastry bag with Crème Pâtissière and fill the pastries. Ice with Glaçage Miroir au Chocolat.

Leslie J. Whipple
Whipple & Wied Catering, Inc.
Lake Oswego, Oregon

CARNE ALLA PIZZAIOLO

I recently returned from Fabriano, Italy where I studied the centuries old heritage of Italian cuisine.

    4 6-ounce slices of beef filet
    3 tablespoons olive oil
    4 cloves garlic, minced
    2 cups tomatoes; peeled, seeded and
        chopped
    4 tablespoons capers, drained
    3 tablespoons Italian parsley, minced
    2 tablespoons fresh oregano, minced
    Salt and pepper to taste

Place beef between 2 pieces of waxed paper and pound until ¼-inch thick. Heat olive oil over medium heat in a large frying pan. Sauté the garlic until fragrant, then add the beef and sauté quickly on both sides. Add remaining ingredients and simmer until beef is cooked and sauce is heated through.

Patricia Wied
Whipple & Wied Catering, Inc.
Lake Oswego, Oregon

PORK TENDERLOIN MEDALLIONS WITH SWEET RED PEPPER SAUCE

1 pork tenderloin cut in butterflied
    medallions
1 cup flour
2 eggs, lightly beaten with 2 tablespoons
    water
1 cup bread crumbs
Salt and pepper to taste
3 tablespoons olive oil

Lightly pound pork medallions with a mallet. Dip medallions in flour, eggwash, then in crumbs. Put coated pieces on a tray. Salt and pepper to taste. Heat oil in large skillet. Sauté in batches until golden brown on each side. Allow 3 medallions per serving. Top with a spoonful of Sweet Red Pepper Sauce (page 141).
Yield: 4 servings.

Tom DeHaven
Fellows House Restaurant and
Inn of the Oregon Trail
Oregon City, Oregon

SWEET RED PEPPER SAUCE

¼ cup olive oil
½ cup chopped onions
2 cups chopped red pepper
2 tablespoons dried basil
2 tablespoons white wine
3 cups tomato concassé, skinned,
    seeded and coarsely chopped

Heat oil, add onions, red pepper and ½ of the basil. Cook over medium heat 10 minutes stirring often. Add wine and reduce over medium-low heat about 15 minutes until thickened. Add tomatoes and remaining basil, stirring often to prevent sticking (about 25 minutes). Puree.
Note: Freezes well.

Tom DeHaven
Fellows House Restaurant and
Inn of the Oregon Trail
Oregon City, Oregon

BILLY BOB'S BUBBA-CUE BEANS

1 1-pound, 13-ounce can Pork & Beans
1 teaspoon dry mustard
1 teaspoon vinegar
1 large onion, finely chopped
4 teaspoons Tabasco
4 ounces ham or cooked bacon, diced
1 tablespoon ketchup
4 teaspoons liquid smoke
1 tablespoon lemon juice
1 medium bell pepper, finely chopped
2 tablespoons dark brown sugar
1 teaspoon Worcestershire sauce
1 teaspoon prepared mustard

Combine all ingredients well and cook in a crock pot on HIGH 3-4 hours.

Robert W. Collins, CEC, CMFP
Collins' Specialty Foods
Portland, Oregon
Miami, Florida

CHIPOTLES CON QUESCO

4 ounces minced bacon
2 to 3 pounds onions, small dice
1 1-pound, 13 ounce can diced tomatoes,
    drained
6 to 10 cloves of garlic, minced
1 16-ounce can green chiles, diced
1 teaspoon cumin
1 4-ounce can Chipotle en Escabeche
    chiles, diced
5 pounds Velveeta cheese, shredded

Render bacon, add onions and cook until transparent. Add tomatoes, garlic, chiles, cumin and diced chipotles. Simmer for 30 minutes, stirring frequently. Add cheese a little at a time until melted and fully incorporated. Serve warm as a dip with tortilla chips. Freezes well.

Robert W. Collins, CEC, CMFP
Collins' Specialty Foods
Portland, Oregon
Miami, Florida

BILLY BOB'S BODACIOUS BANANA BREAD

3 cups whole wheat flour
1 teaspoon salt
1 tablespoon baking powder
½ cup butter
2 cups sugar
1 cup sour cream
4 ripe bananas, mashed
3 tablespoons vanilla
2 cups pecan pieces

Sift together flour, salt and baking powder. Cream together butter and sugar. Mix together sour cream, bananas, vanilla and pecans. Add banana mixture to creamed sugar and butter. Mix well. Add flour mixture one-third at a time, mixing to incorporate after each addition. Bake at 350 degrees until knife inserted in middle comes out clean, about 30 minutes.

Robert W. Collins, CEC, CMFP
Collins' Specialty Foods
Portland, Oregon
Miami, Florida

CHINOOK SALMON WITH HOOD RIVER PEAR SAUCE

My father was Sicilian, and my mother was Indian and Irish. My grandfather, Herbert Picard was a Umatilla Indian (a tribe in Eastern Oregon) who hunted, trapped and fished the great Cellio Falls with spears. A true wilderness man, Herbert taught me how to survive in the woods. My grandmother was Irish and her great-great-grandparents came to Oregon in a covered wagon from Missouri. William McBean, my great-great-great grandfather worked as a clerk at the honorable Hudson Bay Company at Fort Vancouver in 1844.

4 ounces butter
4 6-ounce salmon fillets
Flour for dredging
8 ounces fish stock or chicken stock

Sauce:
¼ cup Riesling wine
1 pear, cored and sliced thinly
1 tablespoon chutney
1 cup whipping cream

Preheat oven to 350 degrees. In skillet, heat butter until it melts but does not turn brown. Dredge salmon fillets in flour and place in skillet skin side up first. Cook until brown and turn fish over to cook 2 minutes. Drain off excess butter and add stock. Place in oven to bake for 8 minutes. While fish is baking make sauce.

In another skillet add wine and pears. Cook until wine is almost gone and add cream and chutney. Reduce until cream coats a spoon and the color is a light caramel color. Place sauce on plate and place salmon on sauce. Garnish with fresh dill sprig.

Anthony J. Danna, Chef
Amadeus
Lake Oswego, Oregon

APLETS

From My Great Grandmother's Recipe Book.

1¼ cups apple; peeled, cored and grated
2 tablespoons unflavored gelatin
2 cups granulated sugar
1 teaspoon lemon juice
1 cup walnuts, chopped
1 teaspoon vanilla
½ cup powdered sugar
1 tablespoon cornstarch

Put ¾ cup grated apple and gelatin in a bowl and set aside. Let stand 10 minutes. In saucepan place remaining grated apples, sugar and lemon juice. Stir until sugar is dissolved. Bring to a boil. Add the apple gelatin mixture. Lower heat and let simmer for 15 minutes (no longer). Stir occasionally, making sure sugar crystals are dissolved. (Dip spatula in water and go around pan to get sugar crystals in pan.) Remove from heat and let stand for 30 minutes.

Add chopped nuts and vanilla. Place in oiled 8 inch pan and refrigerate for 24 hours. Mix together powdered sugar and cornstarch. Cut in bite size pieces and roll in powdered sugar-cornstarch mixture.

Anthony J. Danna, Chef
Amadeus
Lake Oswego,
Oregon

COLUMBIA RIVER STURGEON WITH HAZELNUT HERB BUTTER

4 6-ounce sturgeon fillets
¼ cup flour
¼ cup olive oil
2 tablespoons chopped shallots
1 cup white wine
¼ cup chopped hazelnuts
½ pound butter
¼ cup chopped fresh herbs (dill, basil, tarragon, cilantro or any combination you prefer)

In sauté pan, place enough oil to coat, preheat pan until oil is almost smoking but not quite. Add more oil. Place fillets in flour and coat lightly on both sides, place in pan to cook. Sear fillets and turn. Reduce heat until fish is firm to the touch. Remove fish and keep warm. Pour out oil and place back on heat. Add shallots and deglaze with white wine. Reduce by two-thirds. Add hazelnuts and simmer for a moment. Whisk in butter. Remove from stove, add herbs and let stand for 2 minutes. Spoon over fish and serve. Garnish with some whole herbs and lemon.
Serves 4.

Fred A. Allen, Sous Chef
Waverly Country Club
Milwaukie, Oregon

RED CURRANT BISCUITS

1 pound 2 ounces sifted flour
2 ounces powdered sugar
Pinch salt
½ teaspoon baking powder
7 ounces butter
3 eggs
½ cup buttermilk
½ cup red currants

Mix flour, sugar, salt, baking powder. Add butter, eggs, buttermilk, currants and form into ball. Roll with rolling pin until about ½-inch thick. Cut out desired shapes or sizes with biscuit cutter. Place in buttered biscuit pan and place in preheated oven at 375 degrees for 10 to 12 minutes or until browned. Serve with favorite jam or jelly.
Yield: 12 large biscuits.

Fred A. Allen, Sous Chef
Waverly Country Club
Milwaukie, Oregon

COLUMBIA RIVER SALMON

8 ounces boneless Columbia River
    salmon fillet
4 ounces white wine
½ lemon
2 ounces butter
2 ounces fresh Oregon bay shrimp
Salt
Pepper
1 ounce Dijon mustard
2 ounces Hollandaise Sauce (page 145)

Poach salmon in covered pan with wine, lemon and butter. Place bay shrimp on top of salmon and cover with mixture of Hollandaise and Dijon mustard. Place under broiler 3 to 4 minutes or until lightly browned. Serve with asparagus and red potatoes.
Yield: 2 servings.

Robert Mager, Chef
Red Lion Jantzen Beach
Portland, Oregon

GRILLED SALMON FILLET WITH CITRUS SAUCE

4 6-ounce salmon fillets, boned and
    trimmed
1 ounce oil (olive or vegetable)
½ cup white wine
1 tablespoon chopped shallot
Juice of large orange, lemon, and lime
½ cup heavy cream
¼ cup butter (unsalted)
Zest of orange, lemon, and lime
Segment of orange, lemon, and lime
Salt and pepper

Rub salmon fillets with oil and place on grill. Cook until flesh gives slightly, being sure to turn periodically. While salmon is cooking put white wine, shallots and citrus juice in saucepan. Bring to boil and reduce heat to simmer. Let reduce until liquid is almost gone. Add cream and reduce until cream is thickened. Add butter, remove from heat and whisk until butter is completely incorporated. Strain and hold.

After fish is done, place on plate with some of the sauce already on it. Arrange segments on side of fish and spoon a little more of sauce on top. Sprinkle with zest and serve. Serves 4.

Fred A. Allen, Sous Chef
Waverly Country Club
Milwaukie, Oregon

PAN FRIED SADDLE OF NORTH STEPPE RABBIT WITH SAGE AND ROASTED GARLIC

8 4-ounce rabbit cutlets from the loin
    (chicken works equally well)
1 cup buttermilk
½ cup red wine or balsamic
    vinegar
¼ cup olive oil
1 teaspoon salt
1 teaspoon white pepper
2 teaspoons chopped fresh sage
2 teaspoons chopped fresh parsley
16 peeled cloves of garlic
¼ cup butter, melted
1 cup flour, seasoned with salt and pepper
¼ cup finely diced tomato
2 tablespoons + 16 leaves chopped
    fresh sage

Combine buttermilk, vinegar, olive oil, 1 teaspoon salt, 1 teaspoon white pepper, sage and parsley. Add rabbit and allow to marinade 12 to 24 hours. Drain off the marinade and save for later use in the gravy. Dredge the cutlets in seasoned flour and pan fry at medium high for 3 to 4 minutes on each side until golden. Remove to a warm holding plate. Roast the garlic in the frying fat until browned evenly. Drain off the fat then add the butter and ¼ cup of the dredging flour, blending the two together to form a roux. When the roux develops a nutty aroma add the marinade and whisk along with the garlic cloves until a smooth gravy forms. Adjust the gravy with a little water if necessary making it fluid enough just to coat the back of a spoon.

To complete the gravy add any accumulated juices from the rabbit cutlets, the 2 tablespoons chopped fresh sage and half of the diced tomato. To plate and present, ladle equal amounts of gravy onto four warm dinner plates. Overlap two cutlets onto each plate and place one garlic clove at positions 12, 3, 6 and 9 on each plate. Top the cutlets with an equal portion of the remaining tomato and two of the sage leaves. Say Grace, pass the sourdough bread and enjoy! Serves 4.

Mark Altstetter, Saucier
The Heathman Hotel
Portland, Oregon

HOLLANDAISE SAUCE

3 egg yolks
Juice of 1 lemon
8 ounces clarified butter
Salt
Pepper
Dash of Tabasco sauce

Place egg yolks into stainless steel bowl with lemon juice. Cook over water bath until it forms a ribbon. Slowly add clarified butter, whisking constantly. Season with Tabasco sauce, salt and pepper.

Yield: approximately 1 cup.

Robert Mager, Chef
Red Lion Jantzen Beach
Portland, Oregon

APPLE AND SUN-DRIED CRANBERRY COMPOTE

This cross-cultural condiment may be prepared with plums, apricots or peaches with pleasant results. While the basis for this warm compote has its roots in chutney, the difference is that the fruit is just heated through to benefit the flavors of the spices and the Northwest fruits.

½ ounce olive oil
¼ cup diced onion
2 ounces vinegar, fruit or balsamic
1½ tablespoons brown sugar
¼ inch piece of canela stick, ground
    (or cinnamon)
1 small piece star anise, ground
1 bay leaf
¼ teaspoon whole coriander, ground
¼ teaspoon allspice, ground
3 tart apples, peeled and diced in
    ⅓ inch pieces
¼ cup sun-dried cranberries
1 peeled and diced poblano chiles
2 to 3 diced red jalapenos

Sauté the onions in the olive oil and add the vinegar, brown sugar and spices. Bring to a boil and simmer to dissolve the sugar. Add the apples, cranberries and chiles, cook until the apples are softened slightly and the cherries are plumped. The apples should remain somewhat crunchy.

Fernando Divina
Casa U-Betcha
Portland, Oregon

HONEY ICE CREAM

4 cups milk
2 cups honey
8 egg yolks
2 ⅔ cups heavy cream

Scald milk and add honey, stirring often, bring the milk and honey mixture up to the boiling point. In a bowl, blend the yolks with the heavy cream. Stirring constantly, gradually add the milk and honey mixture to the yolk mixture. Strain through a fine chinoise or several layers of cheese cloth and chill thoroughly before freezing in an ice cream freezer.

Yield: ½ gallon.

Fernando Divina
Casa U-Betcha
Portland, Oregon

BRAISED LENTILS

2 carrots
2 ribs celery
2 onions, small
Oil for sautéing vegetables
4 ounces bacon, finely minced
1½ gallons chicken stock
2 quarts lentils
1 ham hock or pigs trotter, smoked
2 ounces garlic puree
6 bay leaves
1 tablespoon dried basil
2 teaspoons ground black pepper
1 teaspoon ground cloves
1 teaspoon Worcestershire sauce
⅛ teaspoon ground nutmeg

Rough cut vegetables and pulse in a food processor until finely chopped but not pureed. In a heavy bottom pot, add the oil and render the bacon. Add the vegetables and sauté over a low flame. Add the remaining ingredients. Bring to a boil and simmer gently for 15-20 minutes.

Fernando Divina
Casa U-Betcha
Portland, Oregon

PAPA JOE'S MEAT BALLS

1 pound ground beef
1 pound ground pork
2 eggs, beat eggs in bowl with
    ¼ cup milk
1 small onion, finely chopped
2 teaspoons granulated garlic
1 tablespoon lemon pepper
½ teaspoon salt
1½ teaspoons oregano leaves
3½ tablespoons parmesan cheese
2 tablespoons dried parsley
2 tablespoons olive oil
2 cups dried bread crumbs

Mix all ingredients. Shape into golf size balls, medium size. Place on oiled sheet pan and bake at 350 degrees for 12 to 15 minutes.
    Yield: 35 meat balls.

Joe Parente
Portland, Oregon

PAPA JOE'S SPAGHETTI SAUCE

4 tablespoons olive oil
2 small onions, finely chopped
1 cup red wine
1 29-ounce can tomato puree +
    ½ can water
1 29-ounce can tomato sauce +
    ½ can water
2 bay leaves
2 tablespoons Italian seasoning or
    ¼ teaspoon thyme and
    1 teaspoon sweet basil
2 teaspoons granulated garlic
2 teaspoons oregano leaves
2 tablespoons parsley flakes
2 tablespoons powdered chicken base
Pinch sugar
Papa Joe's Meat Balls (at left)

Heat oil on medium heat, add onions to oil and sauté for 20 minutes. Add wine and sauté another 10 minutes. Add tomato puree, sauce and water and all seasonings. Simmer for 1 hour. Add the browned meat balls and simmer in sauce for 1 additional hour. Sauce should be simmered on medium-low heat. Stir often with wooden spoon.

Joe Parente
Portland, Oregon

TORTADITA DE NUEZ
(Little Nut Cakes)

1⅓ cups toasted and peeled filberts
¾ cup toasted peanuts
1 teaspoon *each* chopped fresh basil,
    Mexican oregano, thyme
    and marjoram
1 tablespoon chopped epazote
    (a Mexican herb)
½ cup minced onion
2 10-inch flour tortillas dried on the
    comal or in the oven and crumbled
2 cups grated asadero, manchego
    or jack cheese
1 teaspoon fresh ground pepper
2 eggs, lightly beaten
Oil for frying

In a food processor, chop the nuts until the size of a coarse meal. Then place in a bowl. With a wooden spoon, stir in the herbs, epazote, onion and tortillas and blend thoroughly. Fold the cheese, pepper and eggs into the nut mixture. Form into 2-ounce patties and cook until golden brown on a comal, griddle or in a cast iron skillet. These may be prepared with virtually any nut and feel free to use your imagination with the herbs. If epazote is unavailable, the cakes are splendid nonetheless. I would suggest serving these with a tomato or tomtillo based salsa with good acidity to counter the density of these "meaty" cakes.

Fernando Divina
Casa U-Betcha
Portland, Oregon

SUGAR COOKIES

1 cup powdered sugar
1 cup granulated sugar
1 cup butter or margarine
1 cup vegetable oil
2 eggs
1 teaspoon vanilla
4 cups flour plus 4 tablespoons (exactly)
1 teaspoon salt
1 teaspoon baking soda
½ teaspoon cream of tartar

Blend sugars, butter and oil together. Add eggs, then flour and rest of dry ingredients. Roll in balls the size of walnuts. Place on cookie sheet. Press with glass, dipped in granulated sugar. Bake at 350 degrees for 8 to 10 minutes.
Yield: 10 dozen.
Note: These freeze well. Also makes a nice gift cookie.

Helen Parente
Portland, Oregon

TILLAMOOK TOAST

1 baguette, 4-inches long, cut lengthwise
2 ounces Oregon shrimp
1 ounce mayonnaise
1 teaspoon lemon juice
1 teaspoon Worcestershire sauce
3 slices of Tillamook cheddar cheese

Slice the baguette in half, also cut some of the crust so as to have a smooth surface. Grill the baguette slices on a flat surface, just enough to brown. Mix the shrimps, mayonnaise, lemon juice and Worcestershire sauce together. Spread the shrimp mixture on the bread and top with the cheese slices. Put the whole sandwich in a hot oven (400 degrees) or under the broiler long enough to melt the cheese. Serve hot.

Urbano A. Salvati, Chef
Waverley Country Club
Milwaukie, Oregon

FILET OF BEEF WITH WILD MT. HOOD MUSHROOMS

On the menu at Chalet Swiss in Welches, Oregon (near the Barlow Trail) since its founding in 1972, this dish has consistently been one of the restaurant's most popular entrees.

8 ounces wild Mt. Hood mushrooms
   (see note)
3 shallots
4 6-ounce slices beef tenderloin
Salt and pepper to taste
All-purpose flour
2 tablespoons vegetable oil
¼ cup butter
1½ cups dry white wine, divided
1½ cups whipping cream
1½ cups milk
1 teaspoon Glace de Viande*
1 teaspoon Worcestershire sauce
1 teaspoon lemon juice

Slice or tear the mushrooms. Chop shallots very finely. Season meat with salt and pepper and sprinkle with a little flour. Heat oil in skillet until it smokes. Sauté meat to your desired liking and remove to a cold plate. Place butter into hot pan, and add the chopped shallots. Sauté briefly until golden. Add mushrooms and sauté briefly. Add 1 cup of wine and cook until reduced by half. Add cream and milk and bring to a boil. Let simmer. Add Glace de Viande and cook until liquid reduces and you have a nice smooth cream sauce. Season to taste with white pepper. Stir in Worcestershire sauce and lemon juice. Add ½ cup of wine and reduce to desired consistency. Pour sauce over the tenderloin and serve with Spaetzle (page 150).

NOTE: Fresh chanterelles or morels (in season) are recommended.

*A concentrated beef stock available at specialty stores, or you may substitute a good quality beef paste or bouillon granules such as the brand Maggi.

Yield: 4 servings.

Kurt Mezger, Chef-Owner
Chalet Swiss
Welches, Oregon

RAINBOW TROUT STUFFED WITH DUNGENESS CRABMEAT

1 tablespoon diced onion
1 tablespoon finely minced carrot
1 tablespoon finely minced celery
1 minced garlic clove
4 tablespoons butter
Splash sherry wine
1 rainbow trout, boned, head removed
1 ounce flour
1½ ounces Dungeness crabmeat
3 tablespoons freshly grated bread crumbs
Salt and pepper to taste

Sauté the onion, carrot, celery and garlic in 1 tablespoon of butter for about 2 minutes. Add the sherry wine. Add the crabmeat and cook for 1 minute. Take the mixture off the fire, add the bread

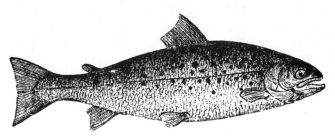

crumbs; salt and pepper to taste. Fill the trout with the stuffing. Dredge the stuffed trout in the flour and sauté with the rest of the butter. The trout may be finished in the oven at 325 degrees for approximately 8 minutes. Serve garnished with lemon, a sidedish of red skinned potatoes and fresh asparagus.

Urbano A. Salvati, Chef
Waverley Country Club
Milwaukie, Oregon

SPAETZLE

Spaetzle in Swiss means dumpling. These dumplings are very small and when sautéd to a golden brown are a delicious accompaniment to any meat or poultry dish.

2 eggs
2 cups all-purpose flour
¾ cup milk
Pinch of sugar
Pinch of pepper
Butter

Mix eggs, flour, milk, sugar and pepper together. Force through a Spaetzle sieve (see note) into a pot of boiling, salted water. When the Spaetzle floats on the surface, remove from the water with a wire sieve. Rinse with cold water and drain well. Sauté Spaetzle in butter until lightly golden brown.

NOTE: If you don't have a Spaetzle sieve, a substitute can be made by drilling ½ inch holes across the bottom of an aluminum cake pan. Push the spaetzle dough through with a rubber spatula. Serve with Filet of Beef with Wild Mt. Hood Mushrooms (page 149).
Yield: 4 servings.

Kurt Mezger, Chef-Owner
Chalet Swiss
Welches, Oregon

BARLOW TRAIL CUSTARD

This popular dessert has been on the menu at Chalet Swiss at Welches, Oregon (near the Barlow Trail) since the restaurant was founded in 1972.

12 tablespoons sugar, divided
½ cup water
1 cup milk
⅛ vanilla bean
3 eggs, beaten
Whipped cream, optional

Put 6 tablespoons sugar and ½ cup water into saucepan and boil until sugar begins to caramelize to a nice golden color. Pour into 4 custard cups, dividing equally. Bring milk, 6 tablespoons sugar and vanilla to a boil. Add to the beaten eggs. Pour on top of caramel sugar in custard cups. Place custard cups in pan with 2-inch high sides. Fill with water until it comes halfway up the sides of the custard cups. Bake in 350 degrees oven for 1 hour. Make sure water in pan does not boil—add cold water if needed. Remove from oven and cool. Refrigerate overnight to liquidize caramel sauce. Serve the following day. To serve, gently cut around edge with knife. Hold top of custard cup with fingers, turn cup upside down and gently remove custard to serving dish. Place whipped cream on top if desired and serve.
Yield: 4 servings.

Kurt Mezger, Chef-Owner
Chalet Swiss
Welches, Oregon

SMOKED TURKEY WINGS

25 turkey wings
4 gallons water
32 ounces salt (4 cups)
24 ounces sugar (3 cups)
16 ounces honey (1½ cups)
36 teaspoons black pepper (¾ cup)
10 each bay leaves
8 ounces minced garlic (¾ cup)

Combine all ingredients and bring to a boil. Cure turkey wings in brine for at least 24 hours, refrigerated. Smoke wings in smoker for 2 hours. Place wings in pan, skin side up, then cover with foil. Put a little water into the pan. Cook wings in 350 degree oven for an hour to an hour and a half or until done. (Remove the foil half-way through cooking process to brown skin.)

David Louis
David Okelberry, Chef
Huber's
Portland, Oregon

MEDALLIONS OF PORK TENDERLOIN WITH HAZELNUTS AND WILD MUSHROOMS

1½ pounds pork tenderloin, trimmed,
    cut into 12 slices
¼ cup flour
Salt and pepper to taste
½ cup olive oil, walnut oil or
    vegetable oil
3 tablespoons chopped shallots
¼ cup madiera wine
½ pound wild mushrooms, any type
    (chanterelles, black trumpet,
    hedgehog, morel) coarsely
    chopped
½ cup chicken stock
½ teaspoon fresh thyme,
    or ¼ teaspoon dry
½ cup hazelnuts, coarsley chopped

Place the pork slices between waxed paper and pound with meat mallet to ¼-inch thick. Salt and pepper pork, dust with flour. In a hot sauté pan, add 1 tablespoon oil and quickly sauté the pork on both sides until lightly brown. Remove the pork and keep warm. Add remaining oil as needed and continue sautéing pork until all pork is cooked.

In the same pan, add the shallots and sauté for one minute, add the wine to the pan, then add the mushrooms, chicken stock, thyme and the hazelnuts. Cook this mixture for about five minutes on medium heat. Adjust the salt and pepper to taste. Return the tenderloins to the pan to reheat. Serve the pork with wild rice or mashed sweet potatoes.

Damon Josephy, Chef
Portland, Oregon

CANTONESE CHICKEN SALAD

Dressing:
½ cup oil
¾ cup rice vinegar
¼ cup soy sauce
¼ cup sesame oil
¼ cup sugar
2 tablespoons black pepper
1 teaspoon garlic powder
1 teaspoon ground ginger

Salad:
3 pounds cooked chicken breast, diced
1 pound water chestnuts, drained and
    sliced
2 cups celery, diced
1 quart lettuce, shredded
1½ cups green onion, sliced
1½ bunches spinach leaves
1 cup pea pods
6 ounces rice noodles, cooked
2 teaspoon nuts

In small bowl, whisk together all dressing ingredients; set aside. In large bowl, combine chicken and the next 4 ingredients. To serve, place 1 ounce spinach leaves on plate. Fan 1½-ounces pea pods on top. Place 5¼-ounces chicken salad in center of plate. Top with 1-ounce rice noodles and nuts. Pour dressing over salad.

Yield: 6 6-ounce servings.

Ron Buzzetti, Chef
Good Shepherd Lutheran Home of the West
Cornelius, Oregon

MIXED VEGETABLE COLESLAW

1 small head of cabbage, shredded
1 large onion, chopped
1 green pepper, chopped
1 red pepper, chopped
2 carrots, grated
3 tablespoons minced parsley
½ cup cider vinegar
½ teaspoon white pepper
3 tablespoons sugar
½ cup safflower oil
½ teaspoon salt

Combine vegetables and toss to mix. Whisk the dressing to blend well and pour over slaw. Cover and chill. Gently toss at serving time. This slaw keeps several days in refrigerator.
Yield: 6 servings.

Ron Buzzetti, Chef
Good Shepherd Lutheran Home of the West
Cornelius, Oregon

LEEK SOUP

2 or 3 leeks, cut up
1 pound potatoes, cut into small pieces
2 slices of bacon
3 cups chicken broth
½ cup milk
2 tablespoons parsley, chopped
Grated cheese, optional

Clean leeks and cut up; use mostly white part and only some of the green. Cut potatoes into small pieces. Cut up bacon and fry, draining excess fat. Add leeks and potatoes and cook for a few minutes. Add broth and some salt and pepper. Simmer covered until vegetables are cooked (about ½ hour). Stir in milk and remove from heat. Sprinkle with chopped parsley and some grated parmesan cheese. If a creamy soup is preferred run in blender after it cools. Reheat but do not boil.

Ken Brace
Bryn Seion Welsh Church
Beavercreek, Oregon

LEEK BROTH

1 quart water
½ pound bacon, diced
2 large leeks
1 pound potatoes
½ pound carrots
1 cup milk
2 teaspoons chopped parsley
Cheese
Salt and pepper

Gently boil the bacon for 40 minutes. Skim off fat. Peel and cut up the carrots and potatoes. Clean and chop the leeks. Add the vegetables to the bacon and simmer until they are tender, about 20 minutes. Add the milk and reheat but do not boil. Add the parsley. Serve with grated cheese.
Yield: 4 servings.

Ken Brace
Bryn Seion Welsh Church
Beavercreek, Oregon

CHICKEN ALLA CACCIATORA
(Hunter-Style Chicken)

2 boneless and skinless chicken
    breasts, lightly floured
¼ cup olive oil
1 tablespoon minced garlic
½ cup minced green onions
½ cup green pepper cut in slices
½ cup mushrooms, sliced or
    quartered—your preference
1½ cups Marinara Sauce (page 153)
½ cup pale dry sherry wine or you
    may use a red wine if you prefer

In a large skillet, lightly brown floured chicken in the olive oil. Remove chicken and set aside. In the same oil, sauté the green pepper, green onions, garlic and mushrooms. Then add the wine and the marinara sauce. Simmer slowly for about 20 minutes on low heat. Serve with rigatoni pasta.

Sylvia Posedel
Sylvia's Italian Restaurant
Portland, Oregon

MOZZARELLA ALLA CAPRESE
(Fresh Tomato, Fresh Mozzarella
and Basil and Olive Oil)

This is one of the most stylish and colorful of Italian appetizers or can be used as a salad.

1 nice large tomato, sliced
Sliced fresh mozzarella
Fresh basil leaves
Olive oil

On a platter or plate, place 1 slice of the tomato, one slice of mozzarella and leaf of basil. Repeat until you've used all the tomato slices and mozzarella. Drizzle with olive oil. Each individual will salt and pepper it according to their taste.

Sylvia Posedel
Sylvia's Italian Restaurant
Portland, Oregon

MARINARA SAUCE

Meatless sauce - keep on hand at all times, it has many uses.

3 tablespoons olive oil
1 tablespoon minced fresh garlic
1 (28 ounce) can crushed Italian
    style tomatoes
1 tablespoon fresh basil or
    ½ tablespoon dry basil
Salt and pepper to taste

Heat oil in skillet and sauté garlic until lightly browned. Add the tomatoes, salt and pepper and basil. Cook uncovered for 20 minutes. Makes about 2 cups.

Sylvia Posedel
Sylvia's Italian Restaurant
Portland, Oregon

WOOD LAND SOUP

My maternal great-great-grandfather, Francis Fletcher, started for Oregon Territory, on horseback, with a group of men in 1839. They arrived in 1840. Francis Fletcher took up a claim between Lafayette (Oregon) and Dayton (Oregon) and was one of the settlers "For Oregon" at Champoeg on May 2, 1843.

My maternal great-great-grandmother, Elizabeth Smith Fletcher (Francis' wife), came to Oregon with the "White Party" in 1842 along with her parents (Andrew and Polly Smith) and brothers and sisters. A family story is that some Indians along the way to Oregon wanted to trade horses for Elizabeth and one of her sisters.

3 tablespoons butter
2½ cups sliced onions
3 cups mushrooms, coarsely sliced
1 to 1½ cups chicken bouillon
⅓ cup filbert butter
Chopped fresh parsley for garnish
Freshly ground pepper

Melt butter in large, deep saucepan over medium heat, add onions and cook until tender and translucent, about 10 minutes. Add mushrooms and cover pan for 5 minutes. Uncover pan, add enough chicken bouillon to cover mushroom and onion mixture, and heat to boiling. Reduce heat and simmer about 10 minutes. Add filbert butter and stir several times, then purée mixture in a blender or food processor, in small batches. Thin soup to desired consistency with hot bouillon. Season and garnish each serving with parsley. This can be made ahead and gently reheated. Makes about 3 cups.

Gayle S. Wilhoit
Henry's Farm
Newburg, Oregon

NORTHWEST SALAD WITH HAZELNUTS
(Salad Dish)

10 ounces fresh or frozen peas
1 cup diced celery
1 cup chopped fresh cauliflower florets
½ cup diced green onions
2 tablespoons chopped pimento
1 cup chopped, roasted hazelnuts
¼ cup crisp, cooked crumbled
      bacon (optional)
½ cup sour cream or yogurt
½ cup ranch style dressing
1 teaspoon Dijon mustard
1 small clove garlic, minced

Rinse peas in hot water or steam (if fresh), drain. Combine vegetables, nuts (and bacon if used) with sour cream or yogurt. Mix dressing, mustard and garlic together, pour over salad mixture. Toss gently and chill.

Gayle S. Wilhoit
Henry's Farm
Newburg, Oregon

FRONTIER HAZELNUT VEGETABLE PIE
(Main Dish)

1 cup fresh broccoli, chopped*
1 cup fresh cauliflower, sliced*
2 cups fresh spinach, chopped*
1 small onion, diced
½ green pepper, diced
1 cup cheddar cheese, grated
1 cup coarsely chopped hazelnuts
1½ cups milk
1 cup baking mix (like Bisquick)
4 eggs
1 teaspoon garlic salt
½ teaspoon pepper

Precook broccoli and cauliflower until almost tender (about 5 minutes). Drain well. Mix broccoli, cauliflower, spinach, onion, green pepper and cheese and put into well-greased 10-inch pie plate. Top with hazelnuts. Beat together the milk, baking mix, eggs, garlic salt and pepper; pour over hazelnuts and vegetables. Bake at 400 degrees for 35 to 40 minutes. Let pie stand 5 minutes before cutting. Serves six.

*Ten ounce packages of frozen, chopped broccoli, cauliflower and spinach may be substituted for fresh. Thaw and drain well. Do not pre-cook.

Gayle S. Wilhoit
Henry's Farm
Newburg, Oregon

CHOCOLATE AND FILBERT BUTTER PIE (Dessert Dish)

½ cup filbert butter
3 tablespoons butter or margarine
1½ cups graham cracker crumbs
Vanilla pudding (recipe below)
Chocolate pudding (recipe below)
Chopped or ground, roasted hazelnuts
   for garnish

Heat ½ cup of filbert butter and butter or margarine until smooth. Stir in cracker crumbs, cool. Press mixture into bottom and sides of 9-inch pie plate. Chill.

Vanilla Pudding:

   3 tablespoons corn starch
   ⅓ cup sugar
   1 egg, beaten
   1½ cups milk, divided
   ¼ cup filbert butter

Mix corn starch, sugar and ¼ cup of cold milk. Scald 1¼ cup milk and add cold mixture gradually to pan. Cook until slightly thickened and add beaten egg. Cook and stir to full boil. Remove from heat and add ¼ cup filbert butter, stirring occasionally to make smooth. Spoon into crust. Chill.

Chocolate pudding:

   2½ tablespoons corn starch
   ½ cup sugar
   1½ ounces chocolate (unsweetened)
   1½ cups milk, divided
   1 teaspoon vanilla

Mix corn starch, sugar and ¼ cup cold milk. Scald 1½ ounces chocolate and 1¼ cup milk (when melted, beat with mixer until smooth). Add cool mixture gradually to pan and cook and stir until full boil is reached. Remove from heat and stir in vanilla. Spoon over vanilla pudding layer, add ground or chopped hazelnuts and chill.

Gayle S. Wilhoit
Henry's Farm
Newburg, Oregon

BOB'S LAMB STEW

Flagstaff Hill gave immigrants their first glimpse of the promise of Oregon, with her fertile valleys and wooded mountains. Down in the valley they saw a lone pine tree, marking the campsight for the weary travelers. The Oregon Trail Bed & Breakfast is nestled below that hill and south of where the lone pine stood.

   2 pounds lamb for stewing (cut up
      lamb shanks or substitute beef)
   ¼ cup flour
   1½ teaspoons salt
   ½ teaspoon Accent
   ¼ teaspoon pepper
   ⅛ teaspoon thyme
   3 tablespoons fat or oil
   2 cups hot water
   1 bay leaf
   1 teaspoon salt
   6 small onions
   6 small whole carrots
   6 potatoes, quartered
   1 cup peas
   1 cup (8 ounce can) tomato sauce

To coat evenly, shake meat pieces in a plastic bag containing a mixture of the flour, salt, Accent, pepper and thyme. Heat fat in a 3 quart top-of-the-range casserole. Add meat pieces and brown on all sides over medium heat, occasionally moving and turning pieces with a spoon. When meat is browned, slowly add the hot water, bay leaf, and thyme. Bring liquid rapidly to boiling; reduce heat, cover and simmer (do not boil) 1½ hours. If necessary, add more hot water as meat cooks. Stir in the 1 teaspoon salt. Add onions, carrots, and potatoes to stew. Cover and cook 25 minutes longer or until vegetables are nearly tender. Mix in the peas and tomato sauce. Cook 10 to 15 minutes, or until meat and vegetables are tender when pierced with a fork. Remove bay leaf before serving.

Marihelen Ciesiel
Oregon Trail Bed & Breakfast
Baker City, Oregon

GOOD RED BEANS
(Extended to 3 meals)

1 pound red beans
1 ham hock (optional)
2 teaspoons dried garlic granules
    (equal amount of garlic,
    2 to 3 cloves)
1 teaspoon salt, without the ham hock
    adjust the salt upwards
½ teaspoon cumin
¼ teaspoon coriander

Wash beans and cover with water until it is about 1 inch above beans. Bring to a boil and boil for 10 minutes. Let set for about one hour until cool, then rinse thoroughly with cold water. Drain off all water. This helps reduce any problems with gas.

Add 7 cups water and the ham hock, if using one, the garlic, salt, cumin and coriander. Cook until tender, 1 to 2 hours. Or use a pressure cooker and set the control at 15 and after it starts to giggle, cook for 45 minutes. Turn off the burner and let it sit until the steam has finished escaping.

Check beans for flavor and adjust seasonings.

First night: Serve these with cornbread or garlic bread.

Second night: Fry up two strips of green pepper in butter. Toast 1 slice of white bread, butter it and quarter. Heat one bowl of the liquid plus a generous amount of beans. Add the green pepper and float the bread on top. You may sprinkle with parmesan cheese.

Third night: Place ¼ cup bacon grease or enough oil to cover in the bottom of a skillet. Add beans and enough liquid to make a paste and fry and mash. Heat home style flour tortillas in a fry pan until they start to puff (to avoid sticking, spray with Pam). Place a row of the mashed beans (fried) down the middle of the shell. Add grated cheese (Monterey Jack and cheddar mixed or for low cholesterol use skim Mozzarella), chopped onions, red chile sauce, chopped tomatoes, guacamole and lettuce that has had a mild vinegar sprinkled on it. Home style tortillas have the best flavor.

Marihelen Ciesiel
Oregon Trail Bed & Breakfast
Baker, Oregon

MUSTARD STEAK

1 round steak
Johnnie's seasoned salt
Yellow American prepared mustard
Garlic Powder

You can purchase pre-tenderized steaks, but they will not be as tender as you can make them. Just lay the steak out on a board and beat it with the back of a large butcher knife. In areas that have the heavy cartilage go ahead and use the sharp edge. Just beat away and enjoy. Then sprinkle both sides of the meat with a seasoned salt, I prefer Johnnie's, and with garlic powder. I use both liberally. Spread a coating of mustard, again on both sides, as though you were putting mayo on bread. Rub all the seasonings into the meat. Use a spray oil to coat the pan and fry on a medium heat till brown. The steak will take quite awhile to fry. This long slow frying (up to about 30 minutes) will help to tenderize the meat.

Marihelen Ciesiel
Oregon Trail Bed & Breakfast
Baker, Oregon

Index

A

Almonds
    Fig Almond Relish   130
Aplets   143
Apple and Sun-Dried Cranberry Compote   146
Apple Butter   109
Apple Snow   62
Apple Tart from Fort Vancouver   92
Apple Treat   97
Apples
    Apple and Sun-Dried Cranberry
        Compote   146
    Apple Butter   109
    Apple Tart from Fort Vancouver   92
    Auble Coogan   61
    Brown Betty   94
    Clara Hawkins Moore's Apple Rolls   3
    Juicy Apple Crisp   91
    Osark Apple Pudding   102
    Sunburst Apple Dumplings   104
Applesauce
    Applesauce Cake with Penuche Icing   71
    Grandma Hatfield's Applesauce
        Fruitcake   68
    Prize Winning Applesauce Cake   56
Applesauce Cake   69
Applesauce Cake with Penuche Icing   71
Auble Coogan   61
Aunt Hattie's Oyster Stew   18
Aunt Inde's Cream Cake   67
Aunt Tillie's Cinnamon Rolls   6

B

Baked Eggplant   25
Baked Halibut with Cheese   39
Baked Salmon with Wild Mushrooms   34
Baked Squirrel   43
Barbecue Beef Sloppy Joes   44

Beef
    Barbecue Beef Sloppy Joes   44
    Beef Stroganoff Family Style   52
    Bison Jerky   48
    Carne Alla Pizzaiolo   140
    Cheddar Swiss Steak   46
    Corned Venison or Beef   47
    Filet of Beef with Wild Mt. Hood
        Mushrooms   149
    Meatloaf   48
    Mother's Oven Stew   50
    Mustard Steak   156
    Papa Joe's Meat Balls   147
    Pot Roast of Beef   49
    Solomi   44
    Standard Beef Hash   51
    Swedish Meatballs   43
Beef Stroganoff Family Style   52
Beet Pickles   110
Beets
    Beet Pickles   110
    Pickled Beets   116
Bernaise Sauce   135
Best Chocolate Pinwheels   79
Best Pan Fried Fish   35
Beurre Blanc Sauce   135
Billy Bob's Bodacious Banana Bread   142
Billy Bob's Bubba-cue Beans   141
Biscuits
    Fried Soda Biscuits   8
    Grandma Hubbard's Baking Powder
        Biscuits   3
    Red Currant Biscuits   144
Bison Jerky   48
Bison Steak   51
Black Bean Soup   22
Blackberries
    Mrs. James W. Cook's Blackberry
        Cake   55
Blackberry Jam Cake   58
Blueberry Pie   88
Bob's Lamb Stew   155
Boiled Icing   55
Boiled Spice Cake   67
Boston Baked Beans   21

Boston Brown Bread 6
Braised Lentils 146
Brandy Sauce 99
Bread and Butter Pickles 110
Bread Pudding with Brandy Sauce 99
Bread Pudding with Lemon Sauce 100
Breads
    Aunt Tillie's Cinnamon Rolls 6
    Billy Bob's Bodacious Banana Bread 142
    Boston Brown Bread 6
    Church Bazaar Doughnuts 11
    Clara Hawkins Moore's Apple Rolls 3
    Crackling Corn Cakes 7
    Dutch Oven Cooking 14
    Fresh Raspberry Tea Bread 129
    Fried Cakes 14
    Fried Soda Biscuits 8
    Gram Bates' Rolls 8
    Grandma Faye's Hot Rolls 9
    Grandma Hubbard's Baking Powder
      Biscuits 3
    Grandma Meacham's Hot Cakes 7
    Hobo Bread 5
    Jolly Boys 10
    Juanita's Spoonbread 138
    Lumber Camp Doughnuts 11
    Maryland Beaten Biscuit 6
    Mom's Buttermilk Huckleberry
      Pancakes 12
    Mormon Johnnycake 9
    Nana's Cornbread 12
    Narcissa's Camp Bread 4
    Noodles 13
    Pinch-Offs 5
    Pricilla's Boston Brown Bread 5
    Red Currant Biscuits 144
    Rhubarb Bread 9
    Scones from Fort Vancouver 14
    Shaker's Cafe Giant Gingerbread
      Muffins 136
    Soda Bread 4
    Sourdough Cornbread 13
    Spider Corncake 8
    Spudnuts 10
    Tea Biscuits 9

    Walnut Cranberry Bread 130
    Whole Wheat Quick Bread 13
Brod Torte 63
Brown Betty 94
Brown Bread
    Boston Brown Bread 6
    Pricilla's Boston Brown Bread 5
Brown Sugar Dumplings 97
Brownies 70
Buffalo
    Bison Jerky 48
    Bison Steak 51
    Sarah Smith's Buffalo Gravy 45
Burnt Leather Cake 65
Burnt Leather Icing 65
Butter Frosting 58

C

Cabbage
    Mixed Vegetable Coleslaw 152
    Stay Crisp Salad 30
Cake Fillings & Frostings
    Boiled Icing 55
    Burnt Leather Icing 65
    Butter Frosting 58
    Miss Tracy's Frosting 63
    Orange Filling 57
    Penuche Icing 71
    Pig Pen Cake Frosting 56
Cakes
    Applesauce Cake 69
    Applesauce Cake with Penuche Icing 71
    Auble Coogan 61
    Aunt Inde's Cream Cake 67
    Blackberry Jam Cake 58
    Boiled Spice Cake 67
    Brod Torte 63
    Burnt Leather Cake 65
    Cheese Cake 61
    Coconut Cake 64
    Crumb Cake 68
    Date Nut Torte 63

Delicious Cake Recipe 60
Dried Apples Fruit Cake 66
Dutch Butter Cake 68
Egg Nog Cake 60
Famous Brownies 66
Gingerbread 60
Grandma Hatfield's Applesauce
    Fruitcake 68
Grandma Meacham's Coffee Cake 59
Grandma Old's Nut Cake 70
Lizzie Robb's Devils Cake 58
Mother's Gingerbread 71
Mrs. Friedlander's Walnut Cake 55
Mrs. James W. Cook's Blackberry Cake 55
Old English Rum Cake 64
Old Raisin Cake 62
Orange Cake 57
Pig Pen Cake from 1880 56
Potato Cake 67
Poverty Cake 62
Prize Winning Applesauce Cake 56
Prune Cake 65
Rose Geranium Cake 66
Walnut Cake 63
Wind Cake 70
Candy
    Aplets 143
    Date Roll 80
    Grandma Winn's French Fudge 82
    Patience Candy 77
    Penuche from Grandma Nahouse 75
Cantonese Chicken Salad 151
Carne Alla Pizzaiolo 140
Cayucas Beans 17
Cheddar Swiss Steak 46
Cheese Cake 61
Cheese Dishes
    Chipotles Con Quesco 141
    Escalloped Cheese and Tomatoes 26
    Savory Coeur À La Crème 139
    Tillamook Toast 148
Cherries
    Maraschino Cherries 113
    Spiced Cherries 116

Chicken
    Cantonese Chicken Salad 151
    Chicken Alla Cacciatora 152
    Chicken Continental 34
    Creamed Chicken 39
    Fried Spring Chicken Southern Style 33
Chicken Alla Cacciatora 152
Chicken Continental 34
Chinook Salmon with Hood River Pear
    Sauce 142
Chipotles Con Quesco 141
Chocolate
    Brownies 70
    Chocolate and Filbert Butter Pie 155
    Chocolate Bread Pudding 101
    Famous Brownies 66
    Lizzie Robb's Devils Cake 58
    Mrs. Emil Frank Em's Chocolate
        Pudding 103
    Upside Down Chocolate Pudding 105
Chocolate and Filbert Butter Pie 155
Chocolate Bread Pudding 101
Christmas Dinner Menu (1909) 33
Christmas Relish 111
Church Bazaar Doughnuts 11
Clams
    Clams Newburg 37
    Minnie Ida's Razor Clam Timbales 35
Clams Newburg 37
Clara Hawkins Moore's Apple Rolls 3
Coconut Cake 64
Cod Cakes with Fresh Applesauce 134
Columbia River Salmon 144
Columbia River Sturgeon with Hazelnut
    Herb Butter 143
Cookies
    Best Chocolate Pinwheels 79
    Gingersnaps 80
    Grandma Goodwin's Cookies 78
    Grandma Senger's Sugar Cookies 75
    Hermits 76
    Honey Clusters 76
    Jumbo Oat Cookies 75
    Lebkuchen 81
    Molasses Cookies 77

Mother's Drop Cookies 80
Oatmeal Cookies 79
Peanut Butter Crisscrosses 78
Shortbread from Fort Vancouver 75
Snickerdoodles 81
Soft Ginger Cookies 81
Sugar Cookies 148
Swedish Spritz 80
Trilbys 82
White Wafer Cookies 82
Corn
Corn Fritters 27
Farmer's Corn Pudding 27
Corn Fritters 27
Cornbreads
Crackling Corn Cakes 7
Nana's Cornbread 12
Sourdough Cornbread 13
Corned Venison or Beef 47
Crab
Crab Leg Sauté 131
Crabmeat Casserole 38
Dungeness Crab Cakes 134
Rainbow Trout Stuffed with Dungeness
Crabmeat 149
Tortelloni with Crab and Gorgonzola 132
Crab Leg Sauté 131
Crabmeat Casserole 38
Crackling Corn Cakes 7
Cranberries
Walnut Cranberry Bread 130
Cream Tomato Soup 22
Creamed Chicken 39
Crumb Cake 68

D

Dad's Oyster Dressing 33
Dandelion Greens Wilted Salad 28
Date Nut Torte 63
Date Roll 80
Dates
Date Nut Torte 63
Date Roll 80

Trilbys 82
Delicious Cake Recipe 60
Depression Sausage 29
Dilly Beans 111
Doughnuts
Church Bazaar Doughnuts 11
Jolly Boys 10
Lumber Camp Doughnuts 11
Spudnuts 10
Dried Apple Pie 90
Dried Apples Fruit Cake 66
Dried Peas & Beans
Billy Bob's Bubba-cue Beans 141
Black Bean Soup 22
Boston Baked Beans 21
Braised Lentils 146
Cayucas Beans 17
Depression Sausage 29
Good Red Beans 156
Grandma Marion's Baked Beans 20
Split Pea Soup 21
White Bean Pie 85
Dry Corn 27
Dumplings 102
Brown Sugar Dumplings 97
Gooseberry Dumplings 99
Rosemabawler 19
Spaetzle 150
Sunburst Apple Dumplings 104
Tomato Stew with Dumplings 18
Dungeness Crab Cakes 134
Dutch Butter Cake 68
Dutch Oven Cooking 14

E

Easter Breakfast 43
Eclairs 140
Edna Norton's Green Tomato Soy 112
Egg Dishes
Easter Breakfast 43
Good Camp Dish, A 45
Ruby Royal 25
Sausage and Egg Bake 48

Egg Nog Cake 60
Eggless, Milkless, Butterless Cake 69
Eliza Oliver's Chess Tarts 87
Emily's Mince Meat 117
Escalloped Cheese and Tomatoes 26

F

Famous Brownies 66
Farmer's Corn Pudding 27
Fig Almond Relish 130
Figs
    Fig Almond Relish 130
Filberts
    Chocolate and Filbert Butter Pie 155
    Tortadita de Nuez 148
Filet of Beef with Wild Mt. Hood
    Mushrooms 149
Fish Chowder 17
Fowl
    Grandma's Chicken and Noodles 37
    Pan Fried Pheasant 38
Fresh Raspberry Tea Bread 129
Fried Cakes 14
Fried Pigs Feet 51
Fried Soda Biscuits 8
Fried Spring Chicken Southern Style 33
Frontier Hazelnut Vegetable Pie 154
Fruit Desserts
    Brown Betty 94
    Grandma Parker's Fruit Soup 19
    Juicy Apple Crisp 91
    Peach Cobbler 92
    Shaker's Cafe Old Time Rhubarb
        Crunch 137
    Strawberry Crumble 94

G

Game
    Baked Squirrel 43
    Gualglie Allo Spiedo 139
    Mother's Oven Stew 50

Pan Fried Saddle of North Steppe Rabbit
    with Sage and Roasted Garlic 145
Gingerbread 60
    Mother's Gingerbread 71
    Shaker's Cafe Giant Gingerbread
        Muffins 136
Gingersnaps 80
Glaze for Baked Ham 45
Good Camp Dish, A 45
Good Red Beans 156
Gooseberries
    Gooseberry Chutney 112
    Gooseberry Dumplings 99
Gooseberry Chutney 112
Gooseberry Dumplings 99
Gram Bates' Rolls 8
Grandma Faye's Hot Rolls 9
Grandma Goodwin's Cookies 78
Grandma Hatfield's Applesauce Fruitcake 68
Grandma Holman's Mincemeat 115
Grandma Hubbard's Baking Powder Biscuits 3
Grandma Hubbard's Top of the Stove Rice
    Pudding 103
Grandma Marion's Baked Beans 20
Grandma Meacham's Coffee Cake 59
Grandma Meacham's Hot Cakes 7
Grandma Meacham's Rhubarb Pudding 97
Grandma Old's Nut Cake 70
Grandma Osie's Raisin Pie 90
Grandma Parker's Fruit Soup 19
Grandma Schweiss's Rhubarb Pie 87
Grandma Senger's Sugar Cookies 75
Grandma Winn's French Fudge 82
Grandma's Chicken and Noodles 37
Great-Grandmother Hovey's Pumpkin Pie
    and Crust 93
Griddle Cakes
    Grandma Meacham's Hot Cakes 7
    Mom's Buttermilk Huckleberry
        Pancakes 12
Grilled Quail with Bacon, Sage and Juniper 139
Grilled Salmon Fillet with Citrus Sauce 144
Gualglie Allo Spiedo 139

H

Hattie's Raspberry Syrup   109
Hazelnuts
      Chocolate and Filbert Butter Pie   155
      Frontier Hazelnut Vegetable Pie   154
      Northwest Salad with Hazelnuts   154
      Tortadita de Nuez   148
Head Cheese   51
Hermits   76
Hobo Bread   5
Hollandaise Sauce   135, 145
Honey Clusters   76
Honey Ice Cream   146

I

Ice Cream
      Honey Ice Cream   146
Irish Colcannon   26
Irish Potato Pudding   100

J

Jalapeno Hollandaise   136
Jam and Preserves   113
Jams & Jellies
      Jam and Preserves   113
      Orange Marmalade   113
      Oregon Prune Jam   129
      Rhubarb Orange Marmalade   116
Jolly Boys   10
Juanita's Spoonbread   138
Juicy Apple Crisp   91
Jumbo Oat Cookies   75

K

Kris' German Potato Salad   28

L

Lebkuchen   81
Leek Broth   152
Leek Soup   152
Lemon
      Cake Fillings & Frostings   92
      Lemon Custard Pudding   98
      Lemon Pudding   100
      Lemon Sour Cream Pie   87
      Lemon Tarts   86
Lemon Cheese Filling   92
Lemon Custard Pudding   98
Lemon Pudding   100
Lemon Sauce   100
Lemon Sour Cream Pie   87
Lemon Tarts   86
Lizzie Robb's Devils Cake   58
Lobster Croquettes   36
Lumber Camp Doughnuts   11

M

Maraschino Cherries   113
Marinara Sauce   153
Maryland Beaten Biscuit   6
Meat
      Pickled Meat   46
      Sarah Smith's Meat Pies   44
Meatloaf   48
Medallions of Pork Tenderloin with
      Hazelnuts and Wild Mushrooms   151
Mincemeat   111
      Grandma Holman's Mincemeat   115
Minnie Ida's Razor Clam Timbales   35
Miss Tracy's Frosting   63
Mixed Vegetable Coleslaw   152
Molasses Cookies   77
Molasses Pudding   101
Mom's Buttermilk Huckleberry Pancakes   12
Mormon Johnnycake   9
Mother's Drop Cookies   80
Mother's Gingerbread   71
Mother's Oven Stew   50